Localized History Series

Teaching History with Community Resources   *Clifford L. Lord*
(Second Edition)   *Series Editor*

STUDENTS' GUIDES   Alabama*   *Charles G. Summersell*
TO LOCALIZED   Alaska*   *Bruce Le Roy*
HISTORY: Arizona   *Madeline F. Pare*
STATES: California   *Andrew Rolle*
                    Colorado   *Carl Ubbelohde*
                    Connecticut*   *Theodore Powell*
                    Delaware   *John A. Monroe*
                    Florida*   *Samuel Proctor*
                    Georgia   *James C. Bonner*
                    Hawaii   *Gerrit P. Judd*
                    Idaho   *Merle W. Wells*
                    Illinois   *Olive S. Foster*
                    Kansas   *Nyle H. Miller*
                    Kentucky   *Thomas D. Clark*
                    Louisiana   *Joe Gray Taylor*
                    Maryland   *Harold R. Manakee*
                    Massachusetts   *William J. Reid*
                    Minnesota   *Russel W. Fridley*
                    Mississippi*   *John & Margaret Moore*
                    Missouri*   *Duane Meyer*
                    Montana*   *Margery Brown*
                    Nebraska*   *Donald F. Danker*
                    New Hampshire   *James Duane Squires*
                    New Jersey   *Richard P. McCormick*
                    New Mexico*   *James T. Forrest*
                    New York   *Marvin Rapp*
                    North Carolina   *William S. Powell*
                    Ohio   *Francis P. Weisenburger*
                    Oklahoma   *A. M. Gibson*
                    Oregon*   *Thomas Vaughan*
                    Pennsylvania   *S. K. Stevens*
                    Rhode Island   *Clifford P. Monahon*
                    South Dakota*   *Herbert Schell*
                    Tennessee   *William T. Alserson*
                    Texas*   *Francis J. Nesmith*
                    Utah   *Everett L. Cooley*
                    Vermont*   *Graham S. Newell*
                    Washington*   *Bruce Le Roy*
                    Wisconsin   *Doris H. Platt*
                    Wyoming   *Lola M. Homsher*

*Titles in Preparation

Localized History Series

CITIES:	Boston*	*Walter Muir Whitehill*
	Chicago*	*Clement M. Silvestro*
	Cincinnati	*Louis L. Tucker*
	Denver*	*John D. Mitchell*
	Houston*	*Joe Frantz & David McComb*
	Los Angeles	*Andrew Rolle*
	Miami*	*Frank Sessa*
	Milwaukee*	*Charles N. Glaab*
	New York City	*Bayrd Still*
	Raleigh-Durham-Chapel Hill	*William S. Powell*
	San Francisco*	*Moses & Ruth S. Rischin*
WATERSHEDS:	The Arkansas*	*Edwin C. McReynolds*
	The Canadian River Valley*	*A. M. Gibson*
	The Cimarron Valley*	*Homer E. Socolofsky*
	The Delaware*	*S. K. Stevens*
	The James*	*Marvin Schlegel*
	The Kansas*	*Nyle H. Miller*
	The Kentucky*	*Thomas D. Clark*
	The Missouri*	*Merrill Mattes*
	The Ohio	*R. E. Banta*
	The Platte*	*James C. Olson*
	The Potomac Valley*	*Walter S. Sandrelin*
	The Sacramento Valley	*Joseph A. McGowan*
	The San Joaquin*	*Andrew Rolle*
	The Snake*	*Merle W. Wells*
	The Susquehanna*	*S. K. Stevens*
	The Tennessee*	*William T. Alderson*
	The Upper Mississippi	*Walter Havighurst*
	Thé Wisconsin Valley	*August Derleth*
PEOPLES:	The Finns	*John Kolehmainen*
	The Germans	*Carl Wittke*
	The Greeks	*Theodore Salutos*
	The Irish	*Carl Wittke*
	The Italians*	*Rudolph Vecoli*
	The Mexicans	*Carey McWilliams*
	The Norwegians	*Einar Haugen*
	The Puerto Ricans*	*Joseph Monseratt*
	The Swedes*	*Franklin Scott*

*Titles in Preparation

MADELINE F. PARE
Chairman, Social Studies Department
Sunnyside High School, Tucson

ARIZONA

A Students' Guide

to Localized History

Teachers College Press
Teachers College   Columbia University
New York, New York

223043

Dedicated to Gerald D. Troester, Ed. D., Educator
Former Superintendent of Sunnyside Schools
Tucson, Arizona

Arizona, A Students' Guide to Localized History
© 1969 by Teachers College, Columbia University

Cover Design by Gaspar Vilato

Library of Congress Catalog Card Number 68-9255

Manufactured in the United States of America

ARIZONA

A Students'
Guide to
Localized History

MADELINE F. PARE

Localized History Series

Clifford L Lord, Editor

 Teachers College Press

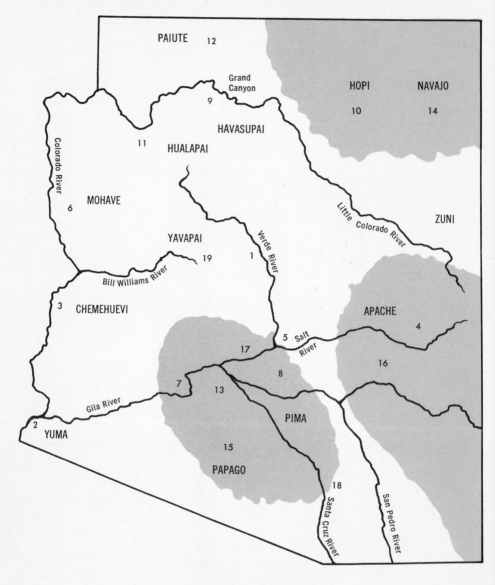

ARIZONA INDIANS

Key to Modern Indian Reservations

1 Camp Verde	6 Fort Mohave	11 Hualapai	16 San Carlos
2 Cocopah	7 Gila Bend	12 Kaibab	17 Salt River
3 Colo. River	8 Gila River	13 Maricopa	18 San Xavier
4 Ft. Apache	9 Havasupai	14 Navajo	19 Yavapai
5 Ft. McDowell	10 Hopi	15 Papago	

From **Arizona Adventure** by Paré and Fireman published by Arizona Historical Foundation, Tempe, Ariz.

Introduction

DO you enjoy a good mystery story? Do you like to follow clues to see where they lead? Do you get a kick out of being a successful arm-chair detective?

If you do, localized history is for you—the story of your own community, what happened, why it happened, and the all-important who made it happen. There is no good textbook, no pat and easy way to find out—you have to do it yourself. And doing it yourself, you find out a great deal not just about your community but about American history, about the great drama of our country's transformation from a transcontinental wilderness into the world's most powerful nation; from a primitive subsistence economy into one producing the world's highest standard of living; from a colonial monarchy (part French, part English, part Spanish) into a democracy where every individual, through the ballot, and freedom of speech, assembly, and petition, has the right to a voice in his government; from a rather rigid society structured on European models into a highly fluid society in which a man can in general rise according to his ability. You discern this easily and dramatically because you see how it happened (and who made it happen) right in your own community.

FIND THE FACTS

How do you (how does the historian) go about it? You can do it yourself, on your own, independently. Or you can cover a lot more ground if you have help in an organized project chosen by your class or undertaken by a history club or group of junior historians such as exists in many states today. After selecting the topic, how do you find out what happened? when it happened? why it happened? who made it happen?

First you want to read whatever is available on the subject. So you go to the library. First your school library, then the public library or the historical society library. You go to the card catalog and look under the subject of your inquiry: Phoenix (Tucson or Flagstaff), or Agriculture—Arizona, or Industrialization—Arizona, or Elections—Arizona, and so forth. The card will look something like this:

Call number   Subject
               Author's name (last name first), birth and death
               years. Title of book. Where published. Date of
               publication: number of pages, Index, if any.

(The call code will differ according to the catalog system your library uses: it will probably be the Library of Congress system; it may be Dewey or even Cutter or, in small libraries, something devised by the local librarian.)

You probably won't find much about your community—or your topic in community history—in books unless a very dramatic event (a Lincoln-Douglas debate at Freeport, Ill., John Brown's raid at Harper's Ferry, a massacre at Mountain Meadow, the battle at the Alamo, etc.) occurred in your community. But there will be one or more county histories that may offer you something useful, perhaps among the paid-for biographical sketches. There may be a local history. Almost certainly there will be some booklets about individual churches, or factories, or clubs, etc., that have celebrated a major anniversary with such a publication. If your librarian thinks it worthwhile, there are available in larger libraries the Library of Congress National Union Catalog for authors and *Book Subjects* for subjects (now printed quarterly, accumulated annually and every five years). The latter gives the title, author, etc., of every book that has been copyrighted within the period covered (the copyright law requires the deposit of two copies of any work copyrighted with the Library of Congress). There are also many specialized bibliographies (listing works on certain general topics or in certain fields) that will be helpful if you are making an exhaustive search.

Then you check the magazines and periodicals. Consult *The Reader's Guide to Periodical Literature* for nonfiction, 1890—date. But remember that many of the magazines it cites will not be available in your library, and few will be worth borrowing on interlibrary loan from major libraries unless the topic clearly covers material you need.

So far, the pickings presumably will have been slim. But now you turn to the newspapers. The local newspaper is the diary of the community, telling day by day (or week by week) what happens (or has happened) in your community. Look for the back files in the historical society, or the public library, or the newspaper office. Here you are apt to strike pay dirt. Inspect the issues covering the period in which you are interested. You will quickly learn how a particular newspaper is made up; where local news appears, where the editorials, the advertisements, the letters to the editor, and so forth—any of which may be useful to your purpose—regularly appear. You'll learn to avoid the "boiler-plate"—the identical ready-made pages that have appeared for some years in many local papers as an economy move. Turn directly to the pages where the sort of material you are interested in appears. Handle them carefully.

Depending on your topic, there are many other places to look for information. If you are working on transportation and its impact on your community, what better place to visit than the railroad offices—to find out what sorts of things in what amounts the railroad brings (and has brought) to the community, what it ships (and has shipped) out to other parts of the country, and what this means (and has meant) to the community's economy? Or the trucking depot, or the freight office, or the lakeside or river or ocean shipping depot? If you are working on the history of mining in your area, what better place to visit than the mining company's office to find out how much ore has been taken in what years from the mines, and what it has sold for, and what this has meant year by year in terms of employment and taxes and income for the community? Or for the story of the community's schools: where better to look than in the offices of the board of education and the superintendent of schools for data on the buildings, curriculum changes, the number of pupils enrolled, and so forth, year by year?

Town (or city) and county records, and the records of state and federal agencies in the county, will also offer significant material for many topics. Census records, land titles in the recorder of deeds' office, tax rolls (which will indicate improvements by sudden rises in the tax return), pension rolls, recreation records, election returns in the town or county clerk's office, minutes of the board of aldermen (or city council), of the board of education and the welfare boards, records of the police department (if available) and the courts, of the water department and the street or public works department, all can offer help on topics that fall under their jurisdiction.

Then there are the resources of your local historical society where there may be manuscripts (letters, diaries, account books, etc.) of importance to your study. Because manuscripts are unique—only one original—the society will want to be sure that you handle them very carefully, may ask that you not use a pen to take notes lest some ink splatter on the manuscript, or may ask you to take other precautions. These may be the letters or diary of some person who had a prominent part in the episode or event you are working on;

they may be the account books of a business venture of critical importance to what you are studying. Be prepared to have trouble reading the handwriting. Have your teacher or father or someone tell you how account books, ledgers, and journals are organized before trying to decipher them.

The society may also have a museum where you can see actual objects related to the events on which you are working. Often actual objects of this sort help you understand something that reading does not make clear. Hefting a tomahawk makes the process of scalping a lot clearer than most texts, just as the cutaway model of an automobile engine make the operations of the piston and the combustion chamber much clearer than any printed description. Old photographs often tell you things that even the newspapers don't mention— about the condition of the sidewalks on Main Street at a given time, or what sort of uniform the police—or the ballplayers—wore, or how things were kept locally in 1870, or what goods the country store sold in 1900.

FILTER THE FACTS

Wherever you look, whatever you do, take notes. Historians have long found that cards (4x6 or 5x8) or half-sheets of bond paper are most useful for note-taking. The card should—like the library card—give the topic: in your case, the phase or part or aspect of the topic the note records. For instance, if your topic is the history of farming practices in your community, your note might be headed "Orchards, 1877," or "Dairying, 1898." You are working on farming, so you need not mention that. Instead, your headline is that phase of farming on which you are taking the note from your research in the library, or at the historical site, or in the newspapers, government reports, an interview.

Next your note should record clearly and specifically what you have just found out. The function of the note is to remind you later when you are writing up a report or working up the class report *precisely* what you have discovered. Finally it should tell you exactly where you found the information —in what book, by whom, when published, and on what page; in what newspaper, of what date, on what page, and in what column; in what letter, in what file, in what historical society; on what trip, to what bank, on what date, by whom you were told what is in your note; on what trip to the railroad yard, on what date, who told you what, etc. The historian, like the lawyer in court, has to be prepared to document his case with footnotes to his sources.

In the process of gathering all your data, you will learn that records disagree on what happened—and why—and to whom. So you will have to learn to evaluate the evidence, just as the judge and jury do in court. Is this a primary (or firsthand) account, or a secondary one recorded later or derived from first-hand accounts often long after the event? Did the man who wrote this letter, or editorial, or diary, or book have an axe to grind? Was he personally involved—or his reputation, or his son, or his fortune? You may even learn that what the textbook says happened in the United States in general did *not* happen in your community—perhaps that quite the reverse occurred. The national generalization is frequently contradicted by the local specific; the local experience may contradict what the teacher says about the broader generalization.

Having found your facts and filtered your facts, you put them together. Here is where the use of topics and dates for headings on your notes is important. They are tools that enable you to organize your data in an orderly fashion by topic and, within the topic, in chronological order. Unless you have been working alone, you have been comparing notes periodically in your class or club, agreeing on new sources to be checked, following through on new assignments. Now with your notes well organized you are ready for the class report or your individual report, oral or written, to tell what you have found out and to interpret it for your colleagues.

FOLLOW THE FACTS

You follow the facts where they lead you. To sound, logical conclusions. Into print in the local newspaper, or in a booklet financed by a local service club, or in the school newspaper, or in mimeographed copies you sell in the community to raise money for still another local historical project. Into setting up a school museum, perhaps making the display cases for the corridors or the cafeteria or basement room in industrial arts classes. Into writing and producing a play or a pageant based on community history. Into putting your knowledge to work, perhaps in cooperation with the local historical society— certainly in cooperation with the city government—in erecting markers at places in the community where history happened. Into getting to appreciate how hard our forefathers worked at what they did, by learning—perhaps in home economics—how to cook in pioneer fashion, how to spin and weave, how to make candles or soap or dyes; learning—perhaps in art classes—how to make dishes or pots or pitchers or block prints. Into folk dances—perhaps in physical education. Into folk fairs and history fairs and radio presentations as a means of sharing your newly won knowledge with your parents and with your community.

In so doing you will gain new insights into our American experiment, new background into how your community has become what it is and into its present problems. You will find many adults eager and willing to help and to add what they can to your projects. You will solve many riddles, learn how rewarding can be the search for answers you don't know to start with and that no textbook and no teacher can tell you, get a head start on techniques that will be highly useful to you in college, or in a trade, or in any business or profession.

In the pages that follow, Madeline F. Paré gives you a useful sendoff with a short history of Arizona to which she has added, period by period, some of the most important books and articles dealing with that period in Arizona, and some of the historical museums and sites, some of the farms and factories and banks and offices you can visit to gain more knowledge of particular activities and their development in your area and community. The possibilities are unlimited. Have fun.

CLIFFORD L. LORD

Hofstra University
February 1969

Contents

Physical Features

A RIZONA is a land of contrasts with an interesting topography. Several times during the ages of its formation it was inundated by shallow inland seas which were repeatedly pushed back by upheaving forces within the earth. Because of these movements, Arizona today offers wide opportunity for geological study. Her lofty peaks, desert ranges and broad valleys are rich in evidence of the cataclysmic events which preceded man's advent. This, according to conservative estimates, occurred at least 15,000 years ago, but in comparison with the previous age of the earth this would be as a dime laid down at the base of the Empire State building. As scientists study the archaeological remains in Arizona, they may be able to push the beginnings of man's occupancy further back in the chronology of history.

The 48th state is one of the fascinating geological laboratories of the world. Hundreds of millions of years of the world's history may be traced in the structure of its rock. Fossils of sea life and amphibians and tracks of reptiles disclose a strange early world of monsters. Only one direct descendant of the dinosaur remains in the area today, the Gila Monster, a poisonous lizard which may now be passing into obsolescence.

Arizona shares with the rest of the American Southwest blue skies, clear dry air, high mountains, deep canyons and rivers which at times run dry. Lying on the western slope of the Rockies, it comprises an area of 113,596 square miles, ranking sixth in area in the United States. From north to south its maximum distance measures 392 miles; from east to west, 338. Utah borders it on the north; New Mexico on the east; Mexico on the south; California and Nevada on the west.

There is some controversy over the origin of the name "Arizona." Perhaps the most widely accepted theory is that it derives from "Arizonac." During the Spanish and Mexican periods the southern part of the present-day state was called the District of Arizonac, of the Province of Sonora, Mexico. The name "Arizonac" comes from two Indian words meaning "the place of the small spring."

This area of little rainfall is a place of unusual scenic grandeur featured by violent contrast. High peaks rise starkly from low desert plains scarred by abysmal chasms that at times channel raging torrents and at others are devoid of water. The low desert in southern Arizona and the high plateau in the north are separated by a massive diagonal mountain zone which stretches from the southeast to the northwest across the state.

The high plateau country in the north is particularly noted for its natural phenomena. It is a land of high mesas and steep canyons. Bare buttes and volcanic cones rise boldly from fields strewn with black cinder-like rocks spewed over them in ages past. Sandstone cliffs of bright coloration make it a wonderland: weird, dramatic, beautiful.

Here an awesome spectacle, the Grand Canyon of the Colorado, has been a lure to millions of visitors. The government has set aside the surrounding area as a National Park. Carved through bright colored rock by the tempestuous Colorado River, the Canyon is in places twelve miles wide and a mile deep. Other Arizona streams have carved canyons but none on such a magnificent scale.

Because of its velocity and its vagaries, this river was able to hold its secrets until the latter half of the nineteenth century. Then an intrepid explorer, Major John Wesley Powell, a one-armed veteran of the Civil War, navigated and charted the Colorado River. He made three scientific expeditions, studying the river, its canyons and their inhabitants, and published his observations. Ever since, valiant men have pitted their strength and ingenuity against the currents and whirlpools of Arizona's greatest stream.

Another scenic wonder in the plateau area is the fantastic and desolate Painted Desert, an area almost devoid of water and plant life. Its sand and grotesquely formed buttes have color and unbelievable brilliance especially at sunset. Close by is the Petrified Forest, comprising 92,000 acres of fallen trees which have been turned into jasper by the action of the elements. The Indians have incorporated the Petrified Forest into their body of legend and the United States government has set the area apart as a National Park.

Although the Colorado is Arizona's greatest river and with its tributaries drains the state, the Gila also has been important historically. Rising in New Mexico, it crosses the entire state of Arizona, emptying into the Colorado. Its valley was one of the dwelling places of early man and it is said to have been continuously occupied for at least 15,000 years. The Gila was followed by mountain men who trapped it for beaver and by missionaries who sought a harvest of souls from the Indian population along its banks. It lured some gold-seekers and it marked a trail used also by traders and soldiers. From 1848 to 1854 it formed part of our international boundary with Mexico. Among Arizona's other rivers are the Little Colorado, Bill Williams, Hassayampa, Verde, Salt, Santa Cruz and San Pedro. Each of these has been important in the development of this land of little water.

The climate of Arizona is as varied as the topography. Temperatures vary according to altitude and there is also a sharp change between day and night. In summer the temperature may reach 120° in the desert lowland, and in winter the high elevations of the mountain zone may register 25° below zero. The annual rainfall in the desert ranges from two to eight inches while the mountains may get as much as thirty inches.

Such variations in land surface and in climate produce marked differences in the vegetation of Arizona. The desert grows seventy-one varieties of cactus, the largest of which is the giant saguaro whose waxen bloom is Arizona's state flower. The barrel cactus, century plant, yucca, ocotillo, cholla and Joshua trees are among the more interesting varieties. Many have brilliant blooms and, set upon a desert carpeted for miles with golden poppies and flowering shrubs and grasses, in spring they make a garden-like scene of exotic beauty. The desert also has its trees. The palo verde, mesquite and ironwood are perhaps the most common of its thorn trees.

Grasses grow abundantly in the mountain meadows which comprise about a quarter of the state's land. This area supports stock raising, an activity which has long had romantic as well as economic implications in the Arizona story. To improve the rangeland over 300 varieties of grass have been introduced to supplement the 89 native grasses. Today dude ranching supersedes stock raising on many Arizona spreads.

Between the grasslands of the mountain meadows and the great spruce and pine forests of the high mountains is a transition zone which in the south supports a scrubby dwarfed type of woodland. This thicket is called chaparral. It consists of manzanita, scrub oak and other broad-leafed varieties. The north piñon-juniper forests thrive in this transition zone. Although the great forests occupy only 9 per cent of the state's land, lumbering is the fourth largest industry in the state. With the most extensive stand of Ponderosa pine in the country, Arizona has the largest molding plant in the world. This type of pine is valuable, also, for cabinet work and plywood, and is used in pulp and paper mills. Because of the wide diversity of its elevations and rainfall, Arizona's climate and vegetation range from Alpine to sub-tropical. While the mountain zone supports trees of great age, the desert plants frequently have frail blooms which live only a few hours.

Animal life in Arizona also shows great diversity. Small animals and rodents frequent the desert while larger animals are found at higher altitudes. Reptiles in wide variety live on the desert, the best known, perhaps, being the rattlesnake which has a fearsome reputation because of its venomous nature. Few humans, however, die from the bite of this snake. Lizards, non-poisonous except for the Gila Monster, abound. A lower order of life on the desert includes the tarantula and other poisonous creatures such as the Black Widow spider, the scorpion, centipede and vinegaroon. Most of these are predatory and live on insects. They have a dense covering for their bodies, yet they cannot survive long exposure to the desert sun, so they are nocturnal in most of their activities.

Arizona's greatest natural resource is her vast mineral wealth which has been of prime importance in the development of the state. Mining has long been practiced. Today this industry brings 600 million dollars annually to the state and the deposits are not yet exhausted. In copper production Arizona leads the nation; it is second in silver, and third in gold. Many other valuable minerals are mined and scientific methods of processing have become a field for the college-trained scientist. With scientific applications have come vast expenditures which take mining more or less out of the hands of private individuals. Big business has entered the field and low-grade rock that would earlier have been considered waste is now processed.

Arizona is fast becoming a mecca for vacationers, health-seekers, retired people and those who enjoy living in the atmosphere of the Old West. With federal assistance, vast installations for water control have been erected. These afford extensive recreation facilities on man-made lakes placed in settings of surpassing natural beauty. Arizona's future as a vacationland seems assured.

Suggested Readings

Corle, Edwin, *The Gila: River of the Southwest* (New York: Rinehart and Co., 1951), a paperback by the University of Nebraska Press, is a combination of geography and history in anecdotal style; Cross, Jack, editor, *Arizona, Its People and Resources* (Tucson: University of Arizona Press, 1960), which deals with the history, land and resources, government and social service, economy, and cultural institutions, was prepared by several University of Arizona professors; Dodge, Natt N. and Herbert S. Zim, *The Southwest: A Guide to the Wide Open Spaces* (New York: Golden Press, 1955); Epstein, Sam and Beryl, *All About the Desert* (New York: Random House, 1957); Federal Writers' Project (revised by Joseph Miller), *Arizona: A State Guide* (New York: Hastings House, 1966) is an indispensable handbook for visitors and newcomers, suggests interesting tours; gives history and legend of many localities; Granger, Byrd H., editor, *Will C. Barnes' Arizona Place Names* (Tucson: University of Arizona Press, 1960), an essential reference book in which place-names have been alphabetically arranged according to the fourteen counties and the Grand Canyon. It has been enlarged from the original, a Barnes' classic, published in 1935, now rare. Kearney, Thomas H. and Robert H. Peebles, *Arizona Flora* (Berkeley: University of California Press, 1960); Krutch,

Joseph Wood, *The Desert Year* (New York: Sloane, 1952) and by the same author are *The Voice of the Desert* (New York: Sloane, 1956) and *Grand Canyon* (New York: Sloane, 1958); Olin, George, *Mammals of the Southwest Deserts* (Globe, Arizona: Southwestern Monuments Association, 1959); In collaboration with Bert M. Fireman, I have written the *Arizona Pageant: A Short History of the 48th State* (Temple: Arizona Historical Foundation, 1967), a general history told in simple prose, designed for the general public and is currently used as a text book in high schools and colleges; Powell, John Wesley, *The Exploration of the Colorado River* (New York: Doubleday, 1961) was originally published in 1875 as a report to the Smithsonian Institution; Wallace, Andrew, editor, *Sources and Readings in Arizona History* (Tucson: Arizona Pioneers' Historical Society, 1965), a checklist of readings, under fifteen headings, each section prepared by a specialist in that area; Woodin, Ann, *Home Is the Desert* (New York: Macmillan, 1964).

PERIODICALS

Some periodicals which are valuable in studying Arizona history:

Arizona and the West, University of Arizona, Tucson (A scholarly journal, issued quarterly); *Arizona Highways,* Arizona Highway Department, Phoenix, a colored pictorial designed for the general public (monthly); *The Journal of Arizona History,* Arizona Pioneers' Historical Society, Tucson, the organ of the Society (quarterly); *Smoke Signal,* Tucson Corral of the Westerners, usually has one rather extensive article (issued at irregular intervals).

Places to Visit

NATIONAL PARKS

Arizona has two National Parks and fifteen National Monuments maintained by the National Park Service, Department of Interior, Washington, D.C. Each of these may be visited by payment of single admission fees, but an annual $7.00 Golden Eagle Passport will admit the purchaser and all who accompany him in a non-commercial vehicle to these and all other National Parks and Monuments as well as many federal recreation areas throughout the United States.

Particular information may be obtained from superintendents located in various areas, namely: Grand Canyon National Park and Grand Canyon National Monument at Grand Canyon, Arizona; Organ Pipe Cactus National Monument at Ajo; Petrified Forest National Park at Holbrook; Pipe Spring National Monument at Moccasin; Saguaro National Monument at Route 8, Box 350, Tucson.

Some National Monuments are administered as a group. Information may be secured from the General Superintendent of Southwestern Monuments, Box 1562 Gila Pueblo, Globe, or from superintendents in the various areas, namely: Canyon de Chelly at Chinle; Casa Grande at Coolidge; Chiricahua at Dos Cabezas; Montezuma Castle at Camp Verde; Navajo at Tonalea; Sunset Crater and Wupatki at Tuba Star Route, Flagstaff; Tonto at Roosevelt; Tumacacori at Tumacacori; Tuzigoot at Clarkdale; Walnut Canyon at Route 1, Box 790, Flagstaff.

Grand Canyon: Magnificent gorge cut by Colorado River. Camping and hotel accommodations on both North and South Rims, the latter open all year, the former from May to September. Administrative services more extensive on the South Rim which has an excellent museum. Ranger-naturalist lectures and sight-seeing trips daily at both rims. South Rim reached by auto from Williams, Flagstaff or Cameron, and by Santa Fé Railroad; North Rim by auto from Jacob Lake.

Petrified Forest: Fallen forest turned to agate by the elements. Museum displaying rock specimens, early animal life of the region and some excellent fossils. Automobile and footpaths through the fields of logs. Contains colorful portion of the Painted Desert. Easily reached from Holbrook. Located on Routes 66 and 260 which are connected by park road.

Chiricahua: Rocky cliffs eroded into weird shapes. Reached from Douglas or Willcox. Steeped in history of Apache Wars.

Organ Pipe Cactus: Unspoiled desert area traversed by a loop road forty miles long. Small museum. Reached from Ajo.

Saguaro: Desert cactus forest. Loop drive. Near Tucson.

Sunset Crater: Cone-shaped extinct volcano distinguished by brightly colored deposits around crater rim, luminescent at sunset. Foot trail to crest 1,000 feet above surrounding country. Fossils of marine life. Interesting lava flow. Near Flagstaff.

SCENIC SPECTACLES

Colossal Cave. Near Vail. Constant temperature 72°. Tours. From Tucson drive out East Broadway to Old Spanish Trail; turn right. Hours: Weekdays 8 A.M. to 6 P.M.; Sundays and holidays 8 A.M. to 7 P.M. Admission: Adults $1.50; children 50¢.

Meteor Crater: Depression 1,000 feet in diameter, 600 feet in depth. Museum and Observatory, 35¢ admission. Can be reached from Winslow or Flagstaff.

Monument Valley: Region of eroded buttes, some hundreds of feet high. Pillars and spires of red sandstone. In northeastern Arizona.

Oak Creek Canyon: Area of brightly colored cliffs. Said to be setting for Zane Grey's *Call of the Canyon.* Trout fishing. Reached from Flagstaff or Sedona by Route 179.

OTHER INTERESTING SIGHTS

Arizona-Sonora Desert Museum: Near Tucson. Unique collection of indoor and outdoor exhibits of plants and animals. Nature trails. Open every day, 9 A.M. to sundown. Admission: Adults, $1.50; military 75¢; children, 6 to 15, 25¢; younger children, free.

Desert Botanical Gardens: Near Phoenix. Unmatched collection of desert plants and succulents.

Buffalo Herds. (Not always visible from the road) At Raymond Ranch on dirt road going off Route 66 about midway between Winslow and Flagstaff; and at South Canyon on dirt road turning south from Route 89, five miles east of House Rock or 33 miles west of Marble Canyon Bridge. Maintained by Arizona Fish and Game Commission. Annual buffalo hunt open to residents of the state with permit. There is a $40.00 charge for buffalo killed, entitling the hunter to head, hide and one quarter of meat.

Papago State Park: Near Phoenix. Cactus plants, fishing ponds, zoo, botanical gardens.

Southwestern Arboretum: Near Florence and Superior. Remarkable collection of plant life.

Rock Collections: "Rockhounds" in almost any locality will advise on rock collecting and choice locations for it. Many rock shops have facilities for making and displaying jewelry using polished native stones.

GEOGRAPHICAL AND GEOLOGICAL CENTERS

The Chamber of Commerce in most communities is a good source of information on the locale. Printed materials available.

Those interested in learning about the area's geology, geography and natural history have the opportunity to do so in the universities. *Arizona State University* at Tempe has a center for Meteorite Studies, featuring Nininger's Meteorite Collection. The Museum of *Northern Arizona University* at Flagstaff features exhibits of rocks, fossils, animals and plants. *University of Arizona* at Tucson has a large exhibit in the Geology Building.

Native Peoples and Their Customs

A RIZONA has been inhabited for over 15,000 years. Evidence of the way man lived through these millennia increases year by year. Archaeology commands widespread interest and the state protects buried evidence by laws against unlicensed digging for relics of the past.

Scientists believe man migrated to the Southwest from Asia via the Bering Strait "bridge." He then presumably drifted southward, hunting as he went, toward a more moderate climate. One site uncovered in southern Arizona revealed an elephant or mammoth skeleton with eight spearheads. At another place, stone butchering tools, spearheads and large animal skeletons indicated that a kill or a feast had been held there by ancient man. Extensive evidence was obtained in Ventana Cave west of Tucson which apparently has been the habitation of man for many centuries. By 2000 B.C., it is believed, man in Arizona had managed to master his environment and had become a food-producer. By the Christian era he led an agricultural life.

Three early cultures evolved in regions of geographical separateness. The people of the desert were the Hohokam: those in the mountains, the Mogollon; and those on the high plateau, the Anasazi. For all of these, as for all who followed them, water scarcity was a common problem.

The Hohokam of the desert were skilled irrigators whose canals spread out in great networks carrying water from living streams. These people developed an artistic pottery which turns up in fragments today. Unfortunately for scholars, the Hohokam cremated their dead, hence knowledge of their physical appearance is unavailable. The most impressive relic of Hohokam culture and evidence of their engineering skill is the Casa Grande Ruin near Coolidge. The federal government has made it a national monument.

The Mogollon people lived to the east and north of the Hohokam. Theirs was a cruder culture. They used the game in their mountains for food and bothered little with agricultural arts. They, however, perfected a stone pipe and practiced basketry and the weaving of cotton cloth.

To the north and northwest of the Mogollon were the Anasazi, the best known of these pre-historic peoples. Since they buried their dead, scientists have a means for studying their way of life and physical appearance. They devised an architecture which accommodated a large population in a small, defensible location, a plan similar to a modern apartment house. The government has set aside as national monuments Montezuma Castle on Beaver Creek, Tuzigoot in the Verde Valley, Tonto near the Salt River north of Globe, and Canyon de Chelly in northeastern Arizona which may be visited. These are extraordinarily well preserved remains of early habitation, some of them of communal type, some designed for separate family living. Wupatki, near Cameron, is another national monument, revealing the way of life in these early days, as are Walnut Canyon in the vicinity of Flagstaff, Navajo in northeastern Arizona and Casa Grande near Coolidge.

By the 1400's, for reasons which have been a matter of controversy, these three great early cultures, the Hohokam, the Mogollon and Anasazi, had gone into a decline. Perhaps war, or a natural catastrophe of wide dimensions produced conditions which reduced the vitality of these early peoples so that they passed into a period of general decline. When the Spaniards came to Arizona in 1540 they found Indians living in scattered communities which differed in custom from one another.

The native population of Arizona in historic times has been categorized according to economy into ranchería, pueblo and band peoples. These divisions coincide generally with linguistic groupings.

The ranchería people, living in scattered settlements in the desert lowlands, were farmers. The pueblo or village people practiced extensive agriculture. They lived on the high plateau in contiguous houses which were several stories high. They followed a rigid religious ritual and, except toward the west, where the Yuman prevailed, they spoke a Ute-Aztecan language. The band people were nomadic farmers who supplemented their diet by hunting. They confined their wanderings, which were usually seasonal, to their own domain. They spoke a language of the Athapascan group. Many other language stocks were in use in the relatively small area which was to become Arizona, and this proved bewildering to the Spanish intruders who became their overlords.

Today Arizona's Indians have become a part of the state's development. Many still live on reservations. The Apaches have an extensive reservation flanking the Salt River and its tributaries in east-central Arizona. The Papagos hold a large area between Ajo and Tucson and a smaller one to the east of it on the Santa Cruz. The Hopi reservation in the northeastern part of the state is entirely surrounded by that of the Navajos. The Havasupais have a tiny reservation within the Grand Canyon. West of them are the Hualapais. The Paiutes live on the Arizona-Utah border in the northwestern part of the state. The Yuma, Cocopah, Chemehuevi and Mohave are along the California border. The Pimas and Maricopas dwell in the Salt and Gila valleys. The Yavapai live in the central mountains and along the Verde. The Zuni are on the New Mexico boundary.

The Arizona Indian tribe best-known to the general public is the Navajo whose homeland is the desolate region of the Four Corners, where Arizona meets Utah, Colorado and New Mexico. The Navajo is handsome, tall and lean. Because of his nomadic heritage, sheep-herding has long been thought of as the Navajo's way of living. He has many taboos which have a profound effect upon his daily life. His religion centers about the medicine man whose art of healing gives him an honored place among his people.

In recent years this tribe has received considerable economic benefit from mining. The Four Corners area has had a history of uranium mining. The first ore used by Madame Curie for the extraction of radium came from there. During World War II this was also the source of the ore used in the experimental work on the atom bomb. The next decade witnessed a uranium boom which outranked the California Gold Rush in prospectors, money and equipment. Since most of the deposits lie in the Navajo Reservation, this tribe received economic benefits from the leasing of the land and also from royalties.

The Hopis live in the same barren region as the Navajos where the dearth of water became the central point of the Hopi religion. This tribe looks toward the past with reverence, cherishing ancient designs in their art and adhering to ancient forms in their pottery which is little short of perfection. They are also skilled silversmiths.

Hopi society is matrilineal and the communal spirit pervades their land. Service to the family, clan, tribe and all other Indians is emphasized. They have lived on the same mesas, dressed in the same costumes, mastered the same arts as did their forefathers. Resistance to the encroachment of other religions has been a pattern in their history.

The most celebrated ancient ritual performed on this continent may well be the Hopi Snake Dance. This ceremonial performance held on one of the sacred hills during nine days of the late summer brings spectators from around the globe. During one part of the ritual, the Snake priests carry live rattlesnakes in their mouths as they move in a circle while others chant prayers for rain.

Arizona has no typical Indian. Each tribe has customs, native ceremonies, religion and lifeway particularly its own. It is in facial appearance that they are similar. All have coppery skin, dark eyes and coarse black hair.

Although many Indians have adopted the way of the white man, tribal relationships remain important and many traditions are deeply rooted.

Suggested Readings

Baldwin, Gordon C., *The Ancient Ones* (New York: W. W. Norton & Co., 1963) describes the development of Pueblo culture in the Four Corners and explains role of archaeologists in interpreting remains of early inhabitants; Cummings, Byron, *First Inhabitants of Arizona and the Southwest* (Tucson: Cummings Publication Council, 1953) describes pre-historic culture of the area; Forrest, Earle R., *Missions and Pueblos of the Old Southwest* (Chicago: Rio Grande Press, 1965, Reprint. Originally published by Arthur H. Clarke, Cleveland, 1929) is a collection of author's observations on missions, Indians, myths, fiestas, legends and ceremonials of the Southwest; Kidder, Alfred V., *An Introduction to the Study of Southwestern Archaeology* (New Haven: Yale University Press, 1924) which gives information on methods and tools of archaeological research is a classic study of Pueblo culture and a later edition (revised in 1962) up-dating original work is available; Kluckholm, Clyde, *The Navaho* (New York: Doubleday, 1962), a revised edition of work published in 1946, is packed with information on all phases of Navajo life; O'Kane, Walter Collins, *The Hopis* (Norman: University of Oklahoma Press, 1964) is a portrait of the Hopis embellished with colored photos; Spicer, Edward H., *Cycles of Conquest* (Tucson: University of Arizona Press, 1963) describes impact of various cultures upon Indians of the Southwest from 1533 and is written from the Indian point of view; Underhill, Ruth Murray, *The Navajos* (Norman: University of Oklahoma Press, 1956) and also *The Papago Indians of Arizona and their Relatives the Pimas* (Washington, D.C.: Department of Interior, 1941) are brief and concise yet penetrating observations on the lifeway of these Indians.

PERIODICALS

An article published in *National Geographic,* May, 1967, vol. 131, no. 5 is useful. The author, Dr. Emil W. Haury, directed extensive archaeological excavations at Snaketown, and his discoveries provide material for this article which is illustrated in color.

The *Arizona Highways* magazine has a wealth of information on the Indians of Arizona. Some issues are devoted exclusively to particular tribes.

Places to Visit

NATIONAL MONUMENTS

Casa Grande Ruins: At Coolidge. Relic of Hohokam culture after it had been influenced by Pueblo migrations. Built about 1300 A.D. Used for only a few generations. Visitors' Center. Guide service, 8:45 A.M. to 4:45 P.M. Nominal fee waived for children under 12 and school groups accompanied by adult.

Canyon de Chelly: On Navajo Reservation. Large cliff-dwellings. Fantastic sandstone cliffs. Contains 300 pre-historic sites and 138 major ruins, most of them inaccessible because of their position high on walls. Self-guiding trails into Canyon and White House Ruin. Rim Tour may be taken in personally owned car any time of year. National Park Headquarters—1 mile from Chinle.

Montezuma Castle: Remains of cliff-dwelling near the Verde River. Largest structure a five-story adobe building in a cave half-way up a sheer cliff. Steps permit inspection. Visitor center. Museum. Nominal fee waived for children under 12 and school groups accompanied by adult. Open 8 A.M. to 5 P.M. Reached from Camp Verde.

Montezuma Well: Well sounded to depth of 55 feet, delivers 1,900,000 gallons of water every 24 hours. Twelve well-preserved cliff dwellings. Remains of pre-historic irrigation system, built 1200 to 1300 A.D. Admission free. On a side road not far from Montezuma Castle.

Tuzigoot: Artifacts displayed at Visitor Center. Dates from 1100 A.D. to 1400. Open from 8 A.M. to 5 P.M. Nominal fee waived for children under 12 or school groups accompanied by adult. Reached from Clarkdale.

Navajo: Three important pre-historic Anasazi ruins and cliff dwellings dating from 12th and 13th centuries. Headquarters at *Betatakin Ruins,* reached by paved road from Route 64, northeast of Tuba City, has visitor center. *Betatakin* cliff dwelling may be seen from a view point an hour's walk from headquarters. Visits to the ruin only with guide, a strenuous climb requiring 3 to 4 hours. *Inscription House,* a ruin of 50 rooms, so named because of the date 1661 which is carved upon it, may be reached by rough road and trail. *Keet Seel,* a ruin of more than 250 rooms built in a cave in a canyon, may be reached by a primitive 8-mile trail on foot or horseback when weather permits.

Tonto: Near Roosevelt Lake in the Salt River Valley. Locale interesting to botanists and ornithologists. Cave-dwelling ruins occupied in the 14th century. Not easily accessible. Visitor Center. Open all year.

Walnut Canyon: East of Flagstaff. Hundreds of small cliff-dwellings built in 11th, 12th and 13th centuries. Open all year.

Wupatki: Group of ruins, some excavated, some restored. Relic of mingled early cultures, dating from 11th century. Visitor center. Open all year. Closed daily at sundown. Reached on side road, off Route 89 between Cameron and Flagstaff.

OTHER INTERESTING PLACES

Besh-Be-Gowah Pueblo: Near Globe. Ruin dating from the 13th century. Museum.

Kinishba Pueblo: Near Fort Apache. Restoration of large prehistoric settlement. Over 700 rooms in several structures. Dates from 12th to 15th centuries. Museum.

Painted Rocks State Historic Park: Near Gila Bend. Outstanding collection of prehistoric Indian writings. Self-conducted tour.

Pueblo Grande: Near Phoenix. A village dating back to the 14th century. Museum and laboratory. Operated by Phoenix Parks and Recreation Department.

MUSEUMS

Arizona State Museum: At University of Arizona, Tucson. One of the world's finest collections on archaeology of the Southwest. Hours: 10 A.M. to 5 P.M. daily. Sundays and holidays 2 P.M. to 5 P.M.

Anthropological Museum: At Arizona State University, Tempe. Exhibits on Indian life of the area.

Museum of Northern Arizona: At Northern Arizona University, Flagstaff. Features exhibits of present day as well as prehistoric Indians. Strong emphasis on the Hopi. Laboratory.

Heard Museum: At Phoenix. Anthropology and primitive arts.

Amerind Foundation Museum: Treasure house of archaeology and anthropology. Open by appointment. At Dragoon.

INDIAN RESERVATIONS

Visitors welcome. Inquire locally as to use of cameras.

For particulars on major religious festivals contact the Chamber of Commerce in a nearby city, as for example: Holbrook or Winslow for information on the dates for the Hopi Snake Dance; Tucson for rituals of the Papagos.

Three Centuries of
Spanish Ventures, 1540-1821

I N a period of restlessness not unlike that of our own times, exploration into
the mysterious Western world and the quest for treasure motivated six-
teenth century men as space travel lures men today. Cabeza de Vaca, a
survivor of an expedition to Florida, after four perilous years of wandering
as a medicine man among many Indian tribes, reached Spanish settlements in
Mexico. There he spread the tale of a fabulous land to the north where cities
flourished. Although de Vaca and his companions likely did not touch soil
which is now Arizona, their tale excited venturesome men, and expeditions set
out from Mexico City to the North.

To map a route for a great scientific expedition scheduled for 1540,
the viceroy sent Friar Marcos de Niza, accompanied by the Negro Estevan
who had been with de Vaca. Though this Franciscan was a seasoned explorer,
his report of the country he crossed was riddled with inaccuracies. The brutal
death of the Negro at the hands of Indians in east central Arizona brought an
abrupt end to the friar's exploration. As his story unfolded upon his return, it
detracted nothing from the alluring prospect of the untold wealth of the Seven
Cities of Gold.

The next year Francisco Vasquez de Coronado set out with an impressive cavalcade for the "fabulous" land with de Niza. As the errors of the
scouting expedition became apparent, the chagrin of the leader and others
forced de Niza to return to Mexico, while Coronado himself sent details in
several directions to search the country for gold. Though spending a fortune
and two years of his life, and journeying as far as the Staked Plains of Kansas,
Coronado found no treasure. His venture was thus counted a failure. His

report of natives, topography, flora and fauna of the region was, however, a vast contribution to the civilized world.

The next penetration of the North came late in the century when mining probes were launched by way of the Rio Grande valley. Small promise of rich returns dampened the interest of the Crown in exploiting the area. The Church, however, hungry for souls, pursued its missionary activities and the king, dutifully if not always generously, supported the effort. As the age of the conquistador with its grandiose dreams faded, the missions became paramount in Spain's assault upon the frontier. Zealous missionaries converted the natives, and in the process extended, defended and pacified the far reaches of Spain's New World Empire. Thus with small outlay, the Crown secured its hegemony over a large area to the exclusion of competing powers.

Three religious orders, Franciscans, Dominicans and Jesuits, participated in this work. Throughout the vast region now comprising California, New Mexico, Texas and Arizona they sought to save souls and implanted the Spanish language, law, culture and religion. In the seventeenth century Franciscans were assigned to New Mexico, northern Arizona and Texas, Jesuits to the Pacific coast of Mexico and Arizona, and Dominicans to Lower California. To aid them the Crown usually placed garrisons in the vicinity of such missions as they built and the civilizing process was thus protected from excessive harassment by "infidel" groups.

In spite of such defensive measures, resistance to Christianity was at times fierce. The Hopi villages in northern Arizona steadily blocked the efforts of the padres. Navajos and Apaches, thus encouraged, rose against the Europeans. Moreover, virtual enslavement of many converted Indians served as a warning against Christianity. In 1680 the Pueblo Revolt in New Mexico spread into northeastern Arizona with blighting effect upon mission activities throughout the region. This uprising, directed by the Indian Popé, mobilized the Indian world against all Spanish policies and people, and for at least a decade it halted Christianizing efforts in New Mexico and Arizona. The Franciscan order suffered the destruction of churches and the murder of many priests. Ranches were raided and hundreds of settlers slaughtered. Every vestige of Spanish Christianity was erased and the natives resumed their former religious practices.

In Pimería Alta, the province south of the Gila and west of the San Pedro, Father Eusebio Francisco Kino, the Jesuit apostle to Arizona's Pima Indians, accomplished his greatest work. There his belief that improved living conditions would promote spiritual gains proved effective. Despite native resistance and government indifference and neglect, he was unswerving in fidelity to his apostolic work. He taught his Indians the fine points of agriculture and established ranches to improve their economic status. His death in 1711, however, left a place which could not be filled and the gains made during his lifetime were soon lost. By mid-century an Indian revolt against Spanish officials struck a heavy blow at Jesuit missions in the land of the Pimas. Quarrels ensued between civil and Church officials as to blame for this uprising and ceased only after a royal mandate to both groups. In 1767 the Jesuits, however, suffered the ultimate blow—expulsion from all Spanish dominions. This drastic act of King Charles III of Spain has ever since been shrouded in mystery. In that day it brought consternation and anguish to many besides the mystified priests who within twenty four hours had to start their exodus to the nearest coastal city.

In Arizona after the Jesuit expulsion, a period of neglect in the missions was followed by the Franciscan take-over. At San Xavier del Bac, the mission established south of Tucson in 1700, Padre Francisco Tomas Garcés established a new pattern in mission work. He lived as an Indian. He spoke to the natives in their own tongue, ate their food and suffered their deprivations. He slept on the bare ground; even learned to think like an Indian, and so he was admitted to the Indian world. A man with an "itchy foot", he traveled widely, visiting the Indians in their rancherías .Wherever he went he carried the banner of Christianity.

In 1774 Father Garcés, in company with a presidial soldier at Tubac, Captain Juan Bautista de Anza, mapped a road from Sonora to the western sea—long a Spanish dream. In the next year he again accompanied de Anza on a major expedition which was to settle San Francisco, California. Garcés and a priest companion stopped with the Yuma Indians to do apostolic work. He traveled, visited and preached incessantly, to make converts for Christianity. Then, in 1781, catastrophe befell him and the mission cause when he met a violent death in the Yuma Massacre. This presaged the loss of Spain's control over this remote frontier. It may even have spelled the doom of Spain in the power struggle of the next century in which she was to lose her New World empire. Had she been able to bind together securely her northern provinces in 1782 she might have been able to resist the later encroachments of Russia, England and the new United States.

The break-down of Spanish governmental control on the frontier was welcomed by the Apaches who saw in this an invitation to raid and pillage. The settlers in the area suffered the ravages which ensued and to some extent a depopulation movement took place. Some hardy individuals took the law into their own hands and met the Apaches with war to the death. Others moved south into more settled regions. From 1785 until Spain was forced to recognize the independence of Mexico in 1821, conditions in these outlying provinces were dependent upon the strength, ingenuity and implacable ferocity of desperate citizens. When independence came it brought no surcease to the holocaust that was the daily ritual of the northern frontier.

Suggested Readings

Bancroft, Hubert Howe, *History of Arizona and New Mexico, 1530–*

1888. (Albuquerque: Horn and Wallace, 1962), a facsimile of the famous 1889 edition, standard work, has excellent material on Spanish period with particularly illuminating footnotes; Herbert E. Bolton has contributed generously to the historical background of literature on Arizona with the following books: *Anza's California Expedition,* (5 vols. Berkeley: University of California Press, 1930–31) contains much material on Spanish Arizona; *Coronado, Knight of Pueblos and Plains* (New York: Whittlesey House, 1949) a thorough study of the Coronado expedition, 1540–42; *The Mission as a Frontier Institution in Spanish-American Colonies* (El Paso: Texas Western College Press, 1962 a reprint) is an exposition of the role of the Spanish mission; *Padre on Horseback* (Chicago: Loyola University Press, 1963 reprint), a tribute to Father Kino; and *Rim of Christendom* (New York: Russell and Russell, 1960. Reprint) is a definitive biography of Kino; Brinkerhoff, Sidney B. and Odie B. Faulk, *Lancers for the King* (Phoenix: Arizona Historical Foundation, 1965), is a study of the military system in the frontier provinces of New Spain; Forbes, Jack, *Apache, Navaho and Spaniard* (Norman: University of Oklahoma, 1960) traces the impact of Spain upon the Indian culture of the Southwest and gives relations of tribes to one another; Horgan, Paul, *Conquistadors in North American History* (New York: Premier Books, 1965) describes the activities of Spanish adventurers in Arizona; Manje, Juan Mateo, *Unknown Arizona and Sonora,* 1693–1721, from the del Castillo version of *Luz de Tierra Incognita:* English translation of Part 2 by Harry J. Karns and associates (Tucson: Arizona Silhouettes, 1954), a translation of diary of Manje, tells of his trips with Father Kino into Arizona; Smith, Fay Jackson, John L. Kessell and Francis J. Fox, S. J., *Father Kino in Arizona* (Phoenix: Arizona Historical Foundation, 1966) describes the explorations and accomplishments of Kino in Arizona. Terrell, John Upton, *Journey into Darkness* (New York: Morrow, 1962), the odyssey of Cabeza de Vaca as told in the original journal; Wellman, Paul I., *Glory, God and Gold* (New York: Doubleday, 1947) gives a picture of the Spanish Conquest.

TRANSLATED DOCUMENTARY ACCOUNTS

Bolton, Herbert E., (editor), *Spanish Explorations in the Southwest, 1542 to 1706* (New York: Barnes and Noble, 1908. Reprinted and available), collection of original narratives of men who explored the Southwest; Coues, Elliot, (editor), *On the Trail of a Spanish Pioneer,* 2 vols. (New York: Francis P. Harper, 1900 Rare), translation of the diary and itinerary of Father Garcés; Hammond, George P. and Agapito Rey, (editors), *Narratives of the Coronado Expedition, 1540–42* (Albuquerque: University of New Mexico Press, 1940); Hodge, Frederick Webb and Theodore H. Lewis, (editors), *Spanish Explorers in the Southern United States, 1528–1543* (Reprinted by Barnes and Noble and is available).

Places to Visit

The Museum of the Arizona Pioneers' Historical Society: Interesting collection of Spanish memorabilia. Displays of armor, weaponry, costumes, religious artifacts, a carreta and a diorama of the walled city of Tucson. A "traveling exhibit" called "Spain in Arizona" traces the story of Spanish Arizona from the Conquest to 1821. It contains weapons, clothing, cooking utensils, pictures and maps. The Society has a wealth of material, books, newspapers, documents, maps, available for research. 949 East 2nd Street, Tucson. No fees. Hours: Monday through Friday 8 A.M. to 5 P.M. Saturday 8 A.M. to 1 P.M. Sunday (winter) 2 P.M. to 5 PM.

Kino Memorial: Block of volcanic rock on which is mounted bronze plate honoring Kino. In downtown Tucson.

San Xavier Mission: Founded by Kino in 1700. Church used by the Papago Indians. Small museum with guided tours to those who request them. Seven miles south of Tucson. Regular Catholic services every Sunday open to the public.

Tubac: Spanish presidial post now a state park. Museum with relics of Spanish times, including maps and documents. Small entrance fee. State park on Route 89 about 20 miles north of Nogales.

Tumacacori National Monument: Ruins of the old mission. Excellent museum. Exhibits and dioramas illustrate the history of the mission and the people of the area. Small entrance fee. Near Tubac on Route 89.

The Mexican Period, 1821-1848

W ITH independence from Spain the Mexican government, unstable and impoverished, had little interest in the pacification of remote regions. As in the latter days of Spanish rule, problems closer to Mexico City held a higher priority. Apaches ran wild in savage depredations upon settlements in the "forgotten frontier." It became evident to the people who lived in these outlying provinces that they could expect no protection from the central government.

The "peace at any price" policies that had been initiated, then abandoned by Spain, had provided food, liquor and weapons for the Apaches. In return, the natives were to live near the Spanish garrisons in peaceful coexistence with the Spaniards. A cynical footnote to this program lay in the belief held by Spain that liquor would have a deleterious effect upon the Indians who in time might thus become less capable foes. The weapons doled out to them were deliberately of a quality inferior to the presidial arms used by Spanish frontier soldiers. Although some years of relative calm had been bought by these subsidies, failure to continue them created bitterness among the native people, resulting in continuous unrest.

To the Apaches, raiding was a way of life. They maintained seven great plunder trails southward for hundreds of miles into Mexico. They usually operated in bands, taking as booty horses, cattle, mules, women, children and church ornaments. Their favorite prey were isolated ranches, unprotected travelers, remote mines. They struck swiftly and as swiftly vanished, leaving demoralization behind them.

Some frontier citizens, disheartened by the neglect and ineptitude of their central government fled for safety; others prepared to exterminate the Apaches and learned to outdo their foes in barbarity. Volunteer units organized and fought the Indians with unparalleled ferocity. Subsidies by provincial governments to Apache hunters made scalp hunting a lucrative trade and bands of considerable size were often organized. When the scalp hunters realized that Mexican and Apache scalps had much similarity, the subsidizing governments attempted to make reservations as to payment. This, however, became a dangerous practice, for the renegades engaged in such hunting were better as allies than as foes. The brutal trade, therefore, continued and some depraved men grew rich on the bounties.

Early in its regime, the new Mexican government had given permission for the opening of a trade route between Missouri and Santa Fé. In 1822 William Becknell took three wagonloads of goods over this trail. He carried such items as cotton cloth, silk, thread, scissors, needles and hardware. His initial success mushroomed and within two years he moved a huge caravan with $25,000.00 worth of goods. It returned with $180,000.00 in gold, $10,000.00 in furs, and many horses and mules.

In spite of the hazards of deserts, wild animals and wilder Indians, many hardy men engaged in trade over the Santa Fé Trail. From Santa Fé, trade routes fanned out to other points. Presently the Santa Fé officials, observing the volume of business, assessed taxes upon the wagons, embittering the traders. The attitude of the traders, frequently deepening into contempt, was often shared by mountain men who plied the streams for beaver. These wanderers in the wilderness were a hardy breed. They frequently disdained the Mexican law which required a license for trapping. They were their own law.

Among those mountain men who trapped in Arizona were Sylvester and James Ohio Pattie, father and son, who came in November 1824 with a wagonload of goods to Santa Fé. They secured licenses to trap beaver and at times had luck in Arizona streams. After many ups and downs, Sylvester died in jail in California and James Ohio returned to the East. There he wrote his *Personal Narrative* which has immortalized his name, for every schoolboy has read of his astonishing adventures in the romantic Southwest. He had the advantage of being the first to write about the area. James Ohio later returned to the West where he died during the California Gold Rush.

Ewing Young, Kit Carson, Paulino Weaver and Old Bill Williams are only a few of the tough mountain men who made history in Arizona. They ventured boldly into wild country, often the first white men to explore it. They were trail-breakers. As they left the last sight of settlement behind, many of them lost any veneer of civilization and became a part of the wilderness. One historian has called them a "reckless breed of men." They learned to read the tracks of any creature, mold bullets from lead bars, strike fire from flint and steel. They slept under the stars and journeyed wherever they wished. Their squaws and children went along or not. The mountain men were self-sufficient.

They were the real pioneers of the Western wilderness.

By 1835 the Mexican government was having serious difficulty with its northeastern province, Texas, which had been colonized by emigrant Americans. The next year a revolt was in full swing. After the Alamo, Goliad and San Jacinto, the Lone Star Republic embarked upon its brief career of independent nationhood under the leadership of President Sam Houston. For the next nine years the petitions of Texas for statehood in the American Union were countered by Mexico's repeated assertion that such annexation would mean war between Mexico and the United States.

When annexation finally occurred in the spring of 1845, the Mexican War ensued. Whether or not it was initiated by some Americans activated by the prevailing spirit of "manifest destiny" remains a matter of debate. While one American army moved on Mexico through Texas another assaulted the heartland of Mexico through Vera Cruz. A third, the Army of the West, under Colonel Stephen Watts Kearny, left Fort Leavenworth, Kansas for the conquest of that desirable province, California. The advance force, which Kearny personally led, went in orderly fashion across the plains to New Mexico.

Arriving in Mexican territory, Kearny encountered little opposition, for his emissaries had preceded him with glowing promises to leading citizens about benefits possible with an American victory. He received the submission of one town after another. The inhabitants seemed to find comfort in the assurances given them by an officer of the United States Army. They had long been neglected by the Mexican government and had been left more or less at the mercy of marauding Indians. Even some Indian chieftains were willing to secure such blessings as they could from this beneficent agent of a great rich government.

Santa Fé fell without a blow, the Mexican officials there having abandoned their posts. Citizens of the town, particularly the merchants, were optimistic over the visit of an Army whose purchases would fill their coffers. Thus, Kearny's take-over was successful and he left Santa Fé with a contingent of regular dragoons for the march across the wilderness to California.

As he proceeded down the Rio Grande Valley he met the famed scout, Kit Carson, eastbound with messages for the government in Washington. Kearny secured his services as guide through the land of the Apaches in spite of Carson's reluctance to recross the dangerous area he had just successfully negotiated. Although progress was slow and perils numerous, this army crossed Arizona along the banks of the Gila. Reaching California the force was engaged in battle by the Californians, but with the help of other American forces already there, the area came under United States control.

The second detachment of Kearny's army was less fleet than the advance group. Included in this slower group was the Mormon Battalion which had enlisted for a year. Arriving in Santa Fé, this contingent went under the command of Captain Philip St. George Cooke, a brilliant organizer who excluded from the group all those he considered liabilities for the difficult march ahead.

Cooke's orders were to map out a wagon road by which army supplies could be shipped to California. He set out with 397 men, five women and twenty-four wagons, with veteran mountain men serving as guides. He crossed into Arizona near Guadalupe Pass negotiating a route hazardous in the extreme. When he came to the old San Bernardino Rancho near present day Douglas he replenished his larders with beef from herds running wild. Along the San Pedro near Benson the army was attacked by wild bulls in an action which has been called the "Battle of the Bulls," reputedly the only battle in which the Mormon Battalion engaged during the war.

Some distance outside of Tucson, emissaries from the officials there asked Cooke not to bring his army into Tucson which was not a military objective. Cooke refused this request because, as he told them, he needed to replenish his supplies. Although he expected a fight in the little city on the Santa Cruz, when he got there the officials had fled. The Tucson residents were respectful and after two days Cooke left for the Gila River route.

The trail took him across the waterless desert where the army suffered great hardships from heat, hunger and thirst. After 102 perilous days Cooke and his detachment safely reached San Diego, tracing a wagon road 1,000 miles long. This road later became a favorite all-weather route to California.

The Mexican War drew to a close with Uncle Sam victorious on all fronts. In the treaty of Guadalupe-Hidalgo the United States received a huge territory including northern Arizona, New Mexico, California, Nevada, Utah, most of Colorado and parts of several other modern states as well as confirmation of its earlier annexation of the Republic of Texas. The new area had an Indian population of 120,000 including many hostiles. One article in the treaty stipulated that the United States was responsible for border peace, and would indemnify Mexican citizens who lost property in Apache raids—a requirement impossible to fulfill. The treaty also required a prompt survey of the international boundary line by both governments.

The treaty was hastily written by men who had scant knowledge of the area. Within a year the United States authorities realized that pacification of the southwestern border was no simple matter. The Apache way of life was based upon raiding and Mexican ranches were an available source of booty. Apache-Mexican hatred was deep seated. Mexican "control" over Arizona had lasted only a quarter of a century. It had been nominal only, for in 1848 Arizona, a wilderness area, was still outside the realm of any functioning governmental supervision.

Books to Read

Blackwelder, Bernice, *Great Westerner, The Story of Kit Carson* (Caldwell, Idaho: Caxton Press, 1962) describes Carson's life as a trapper, guide, soldier and adventurer, covers the early expedition into Arizona with Ewing Young, his role as a scout in the Mexican War, and his career as an army officer in subduing the Navajos; Clark, Dwight L., *Stephen Watts Kearny* (Norman: University of Oklahoma Press, 1961) is one of the few written Kearny biographies; Cleland, Robert Glass, *This Reckless Breed of Men* (New York: Alfred Knopf, 1948) a collection of articles employing legend, anecdote and document about the Santa Fé trade, the mountain men and their philosophy and methods; Cooke, Philip St. George, "Journal", *Exploring Southwestern Trails,* vol. 7. Ralph Bieber, editor (Glendale: Arthur H. Clark Co., 1938), a diary of the first mapping of the first wagon road across Arizona, 1846–47; DeVoto, Bernard, *The Year of Decision, 1846* (Boston: Houghton-Mifflin, 1943) the events of that significant year in which the Mexican War started; Favour, Alpheus H., *Old Bill Williams, Mountain Man* (Norman: University of Oklahoma Press, 1962 Reprint) describes the life of this master trapper; Garber, Paul N., *The Gadsden Treaty* (Gloucester: Peter Smith, 1959), a published doctoral dissertation; Pattie, James Ohio, *Personal Narrative* (Philadelphia: Lippincott, 1962 paperback reprint) is the earliest account of trapping in Arizona by a mountain man; a personal account of the march of the Mormon Battalion written by Tyler, Sergeant Daniel A., *A Concise History of the Mormon Battalion in the Mexican War, 1866–67* (Chicago: Rio Grande Press, 1964 reprint).

Places to Visit

Arizona Pioneer's Historical Society: Diorama which illustrates the departure of the José Romero expedition from Tucson in 1823. Shows the presidio, the settlers and their houses, and the soldiers on their way to reopen the Anza Trail.

Relics from the Mexican period in Arizona are in most of the open collections but because of the brevity of this period, are more or less merged into the Spanish and American periods. Documents, maps and pictures are generally available at all museums and libraries.

From Wilderness to Territory
1848-1863

O NE year after the Mexican War ended, California gold was luring thousands of adventurers across Arizona to *El Dorado*. The Gila Trail was popular because it was usable in all seasons and it saw many kinds of travel by many kinds of persons.

Survey of the international boundary also brought activity into Arizona. The Boundary Commission under John Russell Bartlett was on the scene in 1851. His observations of the geography, flora, fauna and natives of the Southwest provided invaluable information on the area. His *Personal Narrative* is a classic—readable, exciting and carefully illustrated.

Following the border survey, the government sent a group of scientists from the Army Corps of Topographical Engineers to survey a transcontinental railroad route. They studied the lay of the land along the 35th and the 32nd parallels. Captain Lorenzo Sitgreaves marked the route which later was to be used by the Santa Fé Railroad. Lieutenant Amiel W. Whipple followed a path slightly farther to the south. Then Lieutenant John G. Parke came from the West along the 32nd parallel, following the tracks of Cooke's Wagon Road. This activity was undertaken at the insistence of California which had entered the Union in 1850 and was demanding land transportation to the East. Jefferson Davis was Secretary of War and favored the southern route. With the agitation from California backed by the pro-South Pierce administration, the railroad question became a key national issue.

To secure a southerly route, the purchase of an additional strip of land south of the Gila and extending eastward into New Mexico was authorized.

The land of the Gadsden Purchase was described by Kit Carson as an area so desolate that a wolf could not get a living from it. The price was $10-million and the purchase treaty included a clause which released Uncle Sam from the responsibility specified in the treaty of Guadalupe-Hidalgo for pacifying the border area. The new international survey was completed in record time, the American team under Lieutenant William H. Emory, receiving excellent co-operation from the Mexican commissioners.

During the 1850's Arizona was a rugged area. Few people lived north of the Gila. To the south most of the inhabitants were either Indian or Mexican. Disorders were many and the United States government recognized the need for military protection. Within a few years several army posts were established to keep the peace.

In 1849 a camp had been set up on the Colorado River near present-day Yuma to protect Gold Rush traffic. This army post, which went successively by various names, was finally called Fort Yuma. While located on the California side of the river, it served Arizona as well.

Fort Defiance was established in 1851 in the area of the Four Corners to keep the Navajos in check. So desolate was its locality that it was called Hell's Gate by soldiers stationed there.

A third post was on Sonoita Creek in southeastern Arizona about fifteen miles from the old presidial town of Tubac. This installation was to protect mining interests in the vicinity and it was called Fort Buchanan after the President of the United States.

A fourth fort was built on the Colorado River near the head of the Mohave Valley to keep the Mohaves under control. When gold was discovered in this locality late in the decade it became a busy place. This fort was erected at the suggestion of Lieutenant Edward F. Beale who had been commissioned by Secretary of War Jefferson Davis to construct a road from Fort Defiance to the Colorado River. Lieutenant Beale was responsible, also, for the experimental use of camels as pack animals in this road enterprise along the 35th parallel. Although he found the beasts suitable for use in desert country, the army abandoned them shortly, probably due to pressure from the mule lobby.

The year 1857 saw stage coaches for the first time crossing Arizona. The pioneer in this service was the San Antonio-San Diego Mail Line, jocosely called the Jackass Mail since passengers had to ride mule-back for some miles across the western desert. The enterprise was unable to compete with a company beginning operations in the fall of 1858, the Butterfield Overland Mail Line, heavily subsidized for carrying United States mail.

Stage coach travel was a novelty. The coaches were colorful. Transportation, by the standards of the day, was swift. It was, however, uncomfortable and hazardous. Drivers were reckless. Hostiles and renegade whites menaced primitive stations where horses were changed. There, also, travelers were less than "refreshed" by the poorly served and almost never-changing menu of jerked beef, mesquite beans, cornbread and black coffee.

In this same decade some distinguished citizens contributed materially to the development of Arizona. Charles Debrille Poston, in 1854, came with Herman Ehrenberg, a German mining engineer. Poston, believing the place had a promising future in mining, became Arizona's ardent promoter. He secured the capital and organized the Sonora Exploring and Mining Company. The company rebuilt old Tubac and used it as headquarters. It was a Utopia. Of it Poston, years later, said "We had no law but love and no occupation but labor. No government, no taxes, no public debt, no politics. It was a community in a perfect state of nature."

When the Civil War broke out, Poston went to Washington to work for territorial status for Arizona. Several others shared his aspirations and labors. Among them was a dashing West Pointer, Sylvester Mowry, who had been assigned to Fort Yuma, but had resigned from the army to devote his attention to mining interests. Convinced that only organized government could protect the mines from Apache depredations, Mowry urgently appealed to Washington. Receiving scant encouragement there, he turned to the Confederacy which eagerly espoused the cause of territorial status for Arizona. For this defection Mowry was heavily penalized when the Union Army won ascendancy in Arizona.

Samuel P. Heintzelman, also a West Pointer and a commander at Fort Yuma, was another effective advocate of territorial status for Arizona. Although he and others also spent time and energy in the cause, it was Poston who received the accolade as "Father of Arizona." In 1863 these men saw the reward of their labors when Congress established the Territory of Arizona.

Government survey parties, army detachments and exploring expeditions all brought educated men to the wilderness where opportunities for wealth were challenging and life was exciting for the adventurous. Frontier conditions exacted the highest performance from those who came and this had its appeal for the young and ambitious. Typical was Peter R. Brady, an Annapolis graduate, who had joined the Texas Rangers, had served in the Mexican War, had gone west in the Gold Rush and later had joined a survey team in Arizona. He shortly caught the mining fever which was to hold him there all his life. He also maintained an interest in politics and made a continuing contribution to the welfare of Arizona.

As early as 1856, citizens in Arizona were dissatisfied with the lack of protection from Santa Fé, capital of New Mexico Territory. They felt remote from that government's interest. Indeed the residents in the Gadsden Purchase were quite thoroughly isolated by hostile Apaches between them and the seat of government. Citizens living in Arizona, therefore, petitioned Congress to grant a separate civil government for Arizona. New Mexico, in a conciliatory move in 1860, created Arizona County stretching from the Rio Grande to the

Colorado. The dissident groups, however, sought complete separation not only from New Mexico, but from the North as well. After pro-Southern conventions at Mesilla and Tucson, they set up a provisional government and elected a governor, but in the growing tumult of the approaching Civil War this remote government never functioned.

The situation was greatly complicated by the growing resentment of the Indians. Angered by the invasion of their country by white men, they were seething with unrest. Open warfare—the subject of the next chapter—was touched off by an incident in the Sonoita valley, and a holocaust flamed on the Arizona frontier, with the Apaches taking the warpath shortly before the Confederate forces fired on Fort Sumter.

With the Indians ravaging the frontier and a pro-Southern provisional government at least a nominal reality, New Mexico looked like an easy conquest for the South. Early Southern victories enhanced this view, but Union forces were already taking measures to hold New Mexico for the United States. Belatedly, Washington was beginning to see advantage for the Union in the mineral wealth of Arizona, increasingly publicized, as well as the necessity of maintaining overland connections to Southern California.

Shortly after the creation of the Confederate Territory of Arizona on February 14, 1862, the news came to Confederate forces in Arizona that a large California Union Army was getting ready for the reconquest of Arizona and New Mexico. This army, Colonel James H. Carleton's California Column, was no myth. It moved eastward to Tucson where it set up martial law and then on to Sante Fé where Carleton remained in command four years. His rule was harsh but thorough and his methods in subduing the Indians and forcing them into reservations were relentless.

With Union controls established in New Mexico Territory, Arizona's advocates for territorial status resumed their labors in Washington. On February 24, 1863, President Abraham Lincoln signed the document which made Arizona a territory of the United States, separate from New Mexico.

Stories are many as to discussions held and deals made, but regardless of partisan politics, those appointed to the new territorial posts were, for the most part, men of ability. Most of the new officials traveled in a group from Washingon to Santa Fé. There they met Carleton who gave them an escort and considerable advice as to the undesirability of Tucson as a new capital. Its recent sympathy for the Confederate cause as well as its large population of Mexicans were factors in his argument. Carleton's own interest in the protection of mining ventures on Granite Creek weighed heavily in the selection of the unpopulated northern part of the new territory as a place for the new capital.

The governor's party entered Arizona Territory on December 27, 1863. Two days later at Navajo Springs, forty miles west of Zuni, the flag was raised, a prayer was spoken and the oath of office was administered to the new officials.

The temporary capital was to be at Fort Whipple which was under construction. The governor's party went there but when the military post moved that spring to a mining community on Granite Creek, the new government followed. That small settlement became the first real capital of the Territory, and the Secretary of State, Richard C. McCormick, named it Prescott in honor of the great American historian, William Hickling Prescott. Thus was a symbol of culture imparted to a sparsely settled wilderness.

Books to Read

A first-hand account of Arizona in 1850, its flora, fauna, resources and native population was written by Bartlett, John Russell, *Personal Narrative* 2 vols (Chicago: Rio Grande Press, 1965 reprint); Colton, Ray C., *The Civil War in the Western Territories* (Norman: University of Oklahoma Press, 1959) contains a careful account of Arizona's part in the Civil War; Connor, Daniel Ellis, *Joseph Reddeford Walker and the Arizona Adventure* (Norman: University of Oklahoma Press, 1956), journal of the Walker party which discovered gold on the Hassayampa in 1863; Emory, William H., *Lieutenant Emory Reports* (Albuquerque: University of New Mexico Press, 1951), a reprint of the report of Emory to the War Department evaluating the potential of the country as he went westward with Kearny; Foreman, Grant, (editor), *A Pathfinder in the Southwest* (Norman: University of Oklahoma Press, 1914), diary of Lieutenant Amiel W. Whipple who explored for a railroad route from Fort Smith, Arkansas to Los Angeles in 1853–54; Goetzmann, William, *Army Explorations in the American West* (New Haven: Yale University Press, 1959) is an account of several early explorations of Arizona; Gray, Andrew B., *Survey of a Route on the 32nd Parallel for the Texas Western Railroad, 1854.* Lynn R. Bailey, editor (Los Angeles: Westminster Press, 1963) includes the reminiscences of Peter R. Brady; Gressinger, A. W., *Charles D. Poston: Sunland Seer* (Globe: Dale Stuart King, 1961), a biography of Poston who has been called the "Father of Arizona"; Harris, Benjamin Butler, *The Gila Trail,* Richard H. Dillan, editor (Norman: University of Oklahoma Press, 1960) diary of a young attorney who joined a Texas party which followed the Gila Trail to the California gold fields in 1849; Henson, Pauline, *Founding a Wilderness Capital: Prescott, A. T., 1864* (Flagstaff: Northland Press, 1965) is a detailed account of the establishment of territorial government in Arizona; Kerby, Robert L., *The Confederate Invasion of New Mexico and Arizona* (Los Angeles: Westernlore Press, 1958), a tale of a war within a war, General Henry H. Sibley's grandiose dream of extending the Confederacy to the Pacific; Frank C. Lockwood was able to interview many of the individuals mentioned in his book; *Pioneer Days in Arizona* (New York: Macmillan, 1932, rare); Sacks, Dr. B., *Be It Enacted: The Creation of the Territory of Arizona* (Phoenix: Arizona Historical Foundation, 1964) is a penetrating study replete with documents relating to the birth of Arizona Territory;

Sitgreaves, Lorenzo, *Report on an Expedition Down the Zuni and Colorado Rivers in 1851* (Chicago: Rio Grande Press, 1962) was first published in 1853 as *U.S. Senate Executive Document 59.* 32nd Congress, 2nd Session; Tevis, Captain James H., *Arizona in the 50's* (Albuquerque: University of New Mexico Press, 1954); Wallace, Andrew (editor), *Pumpelly's Arizona* (Tucson: Palo Verde Press, 1965) contains excerpts from Raphael Pumpelly's memoirs of Arizona on the eve of the Civil War; Wyllys, Rufus K., *Arizona: The History of a Frontier State* (Phoenix: Hobson and Herr, 1950 rare).

Places to Visit

Arizona Historical Foundation: Arizona State University, at Tempe. Handsome collection of Charles D. Poston's silver.

Arizona Pioneers' Historical Society: At Tucson. Dioramas depicting events in Arizona's early history. Hours: Monday through Friday, 8 A.M. to 5 P.M. Saturdays, 8 A.M. to 1 P.M. Sundays (in winter) 2 P.M. to 5 P.M. No charge.

Fort Bowie: Ruin overlooking Apache Pass Strenuous climb to the fort. Local enquiry for directions.

Mowry Mine: Near Patagonia. Ghost town.

Old Tucson: Reconstruction of Tucson as it was in the 1860's. 13 miles southwest of the city. Used widely as a movie set. Drive out South 6th Avenue to Ajo Way, turn right. Follow signs. Admission: Adults, $1.75; Children, 13-17, 85¢, 6-12, 40¢. Reduced rates for groups.

Pete Kitchen's Ranch House: On Nogales Highway north of Nogales. Many articles of early Arizona days. Kitchen's Boot-Hill Cemetery nearby. Open daily except Mondays. Admission 50¢, children under 12 free.

Picacho Peak State Park: Near Red Rock on the road between Tucson and Casa Grande. Commemorates the camping ground of Mormon Battalion at the Pass in 1846 and a skirmish between Union and Confederate troops in 1862. No charge.

Pipe Springs National Monument: Near Fredonia. Set aside as a memorial to pioneers. Landmark of Mormon history.

Prescott: Many historical sites. Governor's House, built in 1864. Early sessions of legislature were held here. *Pioneer Square,* a group of early buildings within a stockade. *Fort Misery,* two-room log cabin, first house in Prescott. Named for the quality of food provided there when it served as the boarding house of "Virgin Mary."

Quartzsite: In western Arizona. An important stage station during the gold boom. The grave of "Hi Jolly", a Syrian camel driver for the Beale expedition, is located here.

Yuma's Old Adobe: On the Government Grounds in Yuma. Built in 1864 with walls 22 inches thick. Used as quartermaster's depot, barracks and stables in early Arizona.

Most communities of Arizona can boast a collection of pioneer relics which will usually be shown on request. Many place names were given by the surveying teams who traversed the area in the 1850's.

The Indian Wars 1860-1886

W HEN hostilities broke out between the North and the South at Fort Sumter, the Arizona frontier was already ablaze with Indian violence. Many groups of red men were involved in a titanic struggle to wrest from the white settlers land associated with the Indian mores.

The outbreak of the Apaches shortly before hostilities at Fort Sumter between the South and the North precipitated a greater activity of Indian wars on the Arizona frontier, involving at one time or another, many of the tribes, and producing such famed Indian leaders as Cochise and Geronimo.

The situation had been long in developing. Until the Americans became numerous on the Arizona frontier the Indians felt no loss of security. In the 1820's and 1830's, the Americans who went into this wilderness were men on the move—trappers, prospectors, adventurers. Their impact upon the Indian way of life was but fleeting. They doubtless were something of a nuisance to the red man but they were no threat to his existence.

But, after the Mexican War, with the United States undertaking to police the international boundary, life changed for the Arizona Indian. He witnessed the erection of military posts manned by hundreds of soldiers and equipped with large herds of horses. He noticed the influx of settlers who came with their families, animals and wagonloads of supplies and furnishings. He observed with consternation the erection of permanent homes and the fencing of lands which he had always considered his sacred homeland. For him ownership of a parcel of land had no validity. He considered land, like water and air, to be for the common use of all. Confining his living to an area, vague as to boundaries, he yet merged that region in his own identity.

31

The white men who flocked to Arizona in the wake of the Gadsden Purchase were imbued with a vastly different idea of property rights. They had cast their lot in a howling wilderness, for land-ownership or mineral riches, or perhaps only for a new start in life. They drove down their stakes with determination, gathered their herds and prepared to do battle with anyone who threatened their property rights. They were aggressive and competent as individuals and frontier conditions heightened their militancy.

Inevitably the two cultures clashed. As noted in the last chapter, the trouble started with the Apaches. During an Indian raid on a ranch in the Sonoita Valley, the foster son of the owner and some of his cattle were stolen. Blame was placed upon the Chiricahua Apache band of the chieftain Cochise. When protests were lodged at nearby Fort Buchanan a detail under young Lieutenant George N. Bascom was sent to recover the boy and the animals.

The military group camped near Apache Pass and Cochise with some tribesmen came for a visit. When accused of the theft Cochise professed innocence but promised to do what he could to recover the boy and the cattle. Bascom seized six hostages as Cochise departed, some say through a slit in the tent.

Two days later, five hundred warriors were in the vicinity as Cochise came under a flag of truce to demand the return of his tribesmen. He had captives whom he offered in exchange but not the missing boy. The meeting ended in stalemate. A week of savage depredations was climaxed by the killing of both white and Indian prisoners. Cochise, perhaps the greatest Apache chieftain, swore eternal vengeance against every white. For the next twelve years he slaked his vengeance with white blood.

Bascom alone had not been responsible for the decision to hang the Indian hostages but he has been, perhaps unfairly, blamed for the intense savagery which followed. One white man, following this incident, had influence upon Cochise. Captain Tom Jeffords, who ran wagons between Fort Bowie and Tucson even during these terrifying years, became the chieftain's friend, and perhaps as he himself asserted he became this red man's "blood brother." Later on, through Jeffords, the United States government would be able to come to a temporary peace with the Chiricahuas.

During the critical week following the Bascom incident, the Washington government sent orders to post commanders in Arizona to abandon their forts in a consolidation movement that would make soldiers available for the larger war between North and South. This left the frontier citizens at the mercy of marauding Apaches and lawless desperadoes. The Indians believed the withdrawal had occurred as the result of their depredations and that it was a retreat. To them it signalled a chance to regain their homeland. An orgy of pillage and death spread across the Arizona frontier. More than ever, citizens resented the government in Washington, and the Confederacy won adherents.

Arizonans, left to settle their own difficulties, organized Indian-fighting units which became highly effective in their self-imposed task of extermination.

Indian-killing became almost a way of life. Permanent settlers were convinced that they could remain in their new lands only by destroying the Indians. To survive they had to be as bold and tricky as their foes and their guns were always ready for action. The suffering of the settlers during these years knit the white community together and the bond that held them was hatred of the Apaches.

The Civil War in Arizona was virtually over in 1862 with the military take-over by General Carleton, but not the Indian war. To subdue the Apaches and control the renegade whites he ordered the erection of military posts to protect people and property. From his headquarters at Santa Fé he spent some years in subjugating Indians and punishing Confederate sympathizers.

General Carleton early discovered that the Indians did not use his rule book in warfare, and in the fall of 1862, he put into operation a drastic order for the extermination of adult male Mescalero Apaches and Navajos. In this he reflected the sentiments of the pioneer citizens, but it has been suspected that his interest in mining activities motivated this action, for the Indians were a menace to the mines. Carleton felt that confining Indian women and children on reservations would provide training for them which would be conducive to the peaceful exploitation of the Territory.

Carleton sought to subjugate the Navajos as well as the Apaches. With the former he gave Colonel Kit Carson a free hand. Who better than he knew the fortress-like fastness of the Four Corners country? In a relentless campaign, Carson forced the Navajos on the "long walk" to Bosque Redondo, a reservation where Carleton had already placed their enemies, the Apaches. When the latter fled in 1865, the frontier again became a place of terror. The Navajos, released from Bosque Redondo after five years of hardship and disease, returned to their home in the Four Corners.

Plans for pacification of Arizona were high on the agenda of the new Territorial officials. Governor John N. Goodwin toured the territory and enlisted the Arizona Volunteers for a one year term of service. This group never went into the field as a military unit against the Apaches, but it did valiant service in scouting before it disbanded.

In 1865 Arizona was separated from the command of New Mexico and attached to the Military Department of California. Captain John S. Mason was placed in charge of the District of Arizona. Although he reached the area in June he was hampered in his operations by a lack of supplies and of soldiers. The Apaches were running wild, raiding the mails, plundering wagon trains in Apache Pass under the very eye of Fort Bowie. Although Mason set up nine military posts, the district was immense and the roads connecting these forts were the crudest of trails. Citizens were dissatisfied with Mason, feeling that his heart was not in their fight against the Indians, and they clamored for his replacement by a more vigorous Indian fighter. Although Mason and his immediate successors were able to accomplish little in effective warfare against the Apaches, this may well have been due to the handicaps under which they operated rather than to their shortcomings as military men.

When General Edward O. C. Ord took charge in 1869, the pioneers were greatly encouraged. He was vigorous in his campaigns against the Indians and he increased the military posts to eighteen. While the frontier newspapers cheered him, the national press took up the crusade of the humanitarians who called for an end to the slaughter of the Apaches. General Ulysses S. Grant then became president of the United States and instituted his so-called President's Peace Policy.

Ord was removed and his successor, General George Stoneman, was instructed to ease friction between the races in Arizona by putting the Indians on reservations. Meanwhile, he set up temporary feeding stations as a means to relieve tension.

One of these was on Aravaipa Creek near its junction with the San Pedro. About 120 Apaches were living there near Camp Grant. This encampment became the objective of a posse organized in Tucson by citizens enraged by the government's solicitude for the Indians. Composed of ninety-four Papagos, forty-eight Mexicans and six Anglo citizens this company set out, traveling only at night, for the feeding station. Arriving early in the morning, April 30, 1871, they fell upon the sleeping camp with clubs, guns and knives. Of the 108 Indians who were slaughtered 100 were women. Taking twenty-eight children as hostages, the posse returned to Tucson.

Reaction came swiftly in a tirade by the national press which denounced the "unparalleled ferocity and malignity of the massacre." The president was besieged with petitions to save the Indians in the name of humanity. In Arizona, however, the participants in the Camp Grant Massacre were hailed as heroes. Although brought to trial they were acquitted.

In the aftermath, Stoneman was removed and General George Crook was assigned to the vacated post. He was, however, restrained from taking military action until after President Grant's Peace Commissioner, Vincent Colyer, had tried the arts of negotiation with the Apaches. Colyer was assailed in the territorial press as a rascal who deserved to be "stoned to death, like the treacherous, black-hearted dog that he is."

In Washington, rivalry between the departments of War and Interior in the handling of Indian affairs resulted in victory for the latter. The Bureau of Indian Affairs embarked upon a course which sought peace with the Apaches. Following Colyer's suggestion, reservations were provided; the army was to bring the Indians into these designated areas; the hand of friendship was to be extended by the government through economic assistance.

Grant then sent Oliver Otis Howard, the "Christian General", to Arizona to set up these reservations. He met with Cochise who was by this time sick and old and longing for peace for his sorely pressed people. With the promise that his Chiricahuas might have a reservation in their homeland, Cochise agreed to abandon his warfare.

Meanwhile, Crook used the time to study the area and train his men. When Indians broke the peace he used military means to subdue them. He was the greatest of Indian-fighting generals. He understood the Indians and they held him in respect.

During the winter of 1872, Crook intensified his campaign against hostile bands and by spring many surrendered and returned to the reservations. Crook employed Apache scouts to locate and fight other Apaches. He felt great confidence in his scouts, but was later criticized for this policy.

In 1873 the Bureau of Indian Affairs went contrary to Crook's suggestion and concentrated many hostiles on one great reservation on the Gila River. This was also a violation of the agreement which had been made with Cochise for his Chiricahuas. This reservation, San Carlos, was called Hell's Forty Acres by the soldiers who went there. Young John P. Clum, the agent in charge, was fresh from college and filled with ideals and plans by which he sought to improve the lives of his charges. He established an Apache police force for maintaining order on the reservation. Things went along well enough until Crook was transferred from Arizona in 1875. Those officers who succeeded him clashed with Clum, who, after many quarrels, secured the withdrawal of soldiers from the reservation.

In 1876, Geronimo, well-known renegade chieftain, with a hundred followers broke out and blazed a trail of terror through settlements of Arizona, Chihuahua and Sonora. Clum was able, with his Apache police, to effect the arrest of this defiant leader without the help of soldiers, an accomplishment that stunned military personnel.

Clum's career at San Carlos, however, was brief. By 1877 the peace policy had clearly broken down and the army again took charge. Conditions remained so unsettled that in 1882 Crook was reassigned to the ravaged area. Determined to capture or kill the renegades, he scoured the countryside. With the help of his scouts he located the deserters high in the Sierra Madre Mountains of Mexico, barricaded in a natural fortress. He brought them back to San Carlos and there was quiet for two years. Another break then was followed by terrorizing forays by Geronimo and his band. Captured once more in March 1886 the exhausted Indian agreed to return but reneged after he had fortified himself with liquor. Crook, therefore, was embarassed before his superiors who in the dialogue over his methods accepted the General's request for a change in command.

So it fell to another general, after only six months on the assignment, to capture the craftiest and deadliest foe of white settlers in Arizona. General Nelson A. Miles, ambitious and experienced, reaped the benefit of Crook's work. He arrested Geronimo September 3, 1886 and promptly shipped him with his small band to imprisonment in Florida. Miles used an army of 5,000 soldiers to apprehend the tiny band which had diminished to less than forty men, women and children. Arizona from that time on was freed from the harrowing fear of Apaches.

Books to Read

Bailey, Lynn R., *The Long Walk: A History of the Navajo Wars* (Los Angeles: Westernlore Press, 1964) relates the conquest of the Navajos and their plight at Bosque Redondo; Bourke, John Gregory, *On the Border with Crook* (Chicago: Rio Grande Press, 1963, reprint) is an eye witness account; Brandes, Ray, an available handbook on Arizona's military posts is *Frontier Military Posts in Arizona* (Globe: Dale Stuart King, 1960); Browne, J. Ross, *A Tour Through Arizona in 1864* (Tucson: Arizona Silhouettes, 1951, rare reprint), observations of Browne, a sophisticated journalist, who traveled with Charles D. Poston through Arizona in 1864; Cremony, John C., *Life Among the Apaches* (Tucson: Arizona Silhouettes, 1951, rare reprint) describes Apache customs from personal observation; Davis, Britton, *The Truth About Geronimo* (New Haven: Yale University Press, 1963 reprint) is a personal account of a soldier who went into Mexico on an expedition hunting Geronimo; Lockwood, Frank C., *The Apache Indians* (New York: Macmillan, 1938, rare) describes the life way of the Apaches; Miller, Joseph, *The Arizona Story* (New York: Hastings House, 1952), a collection of fast-moving newspaper articles describing early days in Arizona; Ogle, Ralph H., *Federal Control of the Western Apaches,* (1848–1886) (Albuquerque: University of New Mexico Press, 1940), a published doctoral dissertation is the best book on this particular phase of the Apache problem. Summerhayes, Martha, *Vanishing Arizona* (Tucson: Arizona Silhouettes, 1955, reprint), an army wife's account of the life on the Arizona frontier in the 1870's; Thrapp, Dan L., *Al Sieber, Chief of Scouts* (Norman: University of Oklahoma Press, 1964), biography tells the story of the Apache Wars; Wellman, Paul I., *Death in the Desert* (New York: Doubleday, 1934), describes incidents in the Apache Wars.

Places to Visit

Arizona State Museum: On the campus of Arizona University at Tucson. Many exhibits and pictures showing Apache life. Hours: Daily 10 A.M. to 5 P.M. Sundays and holidays 2 P.M. to 5 P.M.

Arizona Pioneers' Historical Society: Excellent diorama of Apache warfare. Many artifacts of that time. 949 East 2nd Street, Tucson. Hours: Monday through Friday 8 A.M. to 5 P.M.; Saturday 8 A.M. to 1 P.M.; Sunday (winter) 2 P.M. to 5 P.M.

Canyon de Chelly National Monument: In northern Arizona. Scene of Carson's triumph over the Navajos in 1863–64.

Cochise Stronghold: On Route 666 in the Dragoon Mountains. For many years the safe hiding place of Cochise.

Fort Bowie: Group of ruins overlooking Apache Pass. Make local enquiry for directions. Strenuous walk up to ruins.

Fort Verde Museum: At Camp Verde, near the Black Canyon Highway about 55 miles south of Flagstaff. Several buildings and many artifacts dating from Apache War period. Admission, adults 25¢.

San Carlos Museum: On the San Carlos Reservation. Small but excellent collection of Apache artifacts.

Years of Development, Social, Economic, Political, 1886-1912

EDUCATION was slow to start in Arizona Territory. Repercussions of the Civil War overshadowed the importance of schooling. Threats of Apache attack made most citizens aware of the futility of schooling where life expectancy had so few guarantees.

In September, 1864 Governor John N. Goodwin asked the first legislature for an appropriation for education. No public school was at that time in operation, but money was given to a small school at San Xavier Mission. Financial encouragement was also given to any town holding classes. When the Civil War ended more attention was devoted to the question of education. In 1867 a law required schools when population warranted them but it failed to include an appropriation of public funds.

In the 1870's substantial gains were made and most of these came through the efforts of Governor Anson P. K. Safford, ever since known as the "father of the public schools system of Arizona." He believed that Arizona could attain stability only through education. Since much of the population spoke only Spanish and had alien traditions, he instituted a program of Americanization.

In spite of opposition among the lawmakers, he wrested from them a meager school law which set up a school system at least on paper. He took his crusade to the people. Dangers of attack did not deter him. He knew how to talk to simple folk since he had himself been a laborer. He inspired all whom he visited with a desire to improve their school, if they had one, or to get one if they had none. He then attacked the problem of getting trained teachers to fill positions on a frontier which offered no guarantees of tenure.

When Safford's second term ended, Arizona had twenty-eight public schools caring for 3,089 students with thirty-seven teachers. Since most of the schools had only one teacher, class loads were tremendous. By 1880, 102 teachers operated schools with a student population of 4,212 pupils. Burdens became great and some buildings had to be closed. Today 675 public schools in Arizona have an enrollment of 391,759 students with 15,435 teachers.

In the nineteenth century a great Catholic priest, Father Jean Baptiste Salpointe, worked with matchless vigor over wide stretches of wilderness to preach his faith. By his zeal he brought schools and also hospitals to several Arizona communities. Today the parochial schools of Arizona and other private schools have a large enrollment. At the elementary level all of these follow the state curriculum and use state-adopted texts. Religious instruction is supplementary in church-supported schools. Kindergartens are generally private enterprises because few communities sustain a public school at this level.

Higher education had its start in Arizona because of the drive and vision of one of its great citizens. Judge Charles Trumbull Hayden, the father of the long-time senior Senator from Arizona, Carl Hayden, became convinced that Arizona would always have teacher shortage until it adopted a teacher-training program. With his backing, a bill creating a Normal School passed the territorial legislature after a stormy debate.

The next year a four-room structure, the Arizona Territorial Normal School, was operating at Tempe with a one-man faculty to care for 33 students. By the end of the century it had graduated more than a hundred teachers and it has been turning them out ever since. Today under the name Arizona State University it operates an extensive program for more than 20,000 students.

The Normal School which opened at Flagstaff in 1899 had much the same kind of a beginning. Thirty-three students enrolled the first year and its faculty numbered two. Today it is Northern Arizona University and its expanding facilities give promise of a bright future for over 6,000 students.

The University of Arizona at Tucson had a reluctant start. Although authorized in 1885, it opened its doors for the thirty-six students of its first class in 1891 with six faculty members, in one unfinished building. Today its enrollment is over 20,000; its research facilities are extensive and varied. It offers a doctoral program in no less than forty-five fields, and it has recently started work on the development of a Medical School.

Interest in higher education has been a continuing attitude in Arizona. Its junior college system is growing and a few independent colleges are also in operation. The educational program in Arizona, initiated under almost incredible hazards, has mushroomed until it has become one of Arizona's great business enterprises. The struggle against frontier odds indeed may have had the effect of enhancing its value. The state's expanding program for its exploding population undoubtedly creates problems for school administrators. The achievements of a vivid past must be their challenge. The citizens of tomorrow have a wealth of educational opportunities and hopefully they have absorbed enough of the pioneer spirit to make good use of them.

Religion also has had a profound effect upon the lives of the citizens of the 48th state. The earliest influence was the Roman Catholic Church of Spain which had a three hundred year advantage over the other Christian churches. The work of such missionaries as the Jesuit Kino and the Franciscan Garcés kindled a responsive attitude toward Roman Catholicism that lives today among many Indian people.

The Mormon Church also has had a vigorous program in Arizona. Missionaries came down from Utah and lived among the Indians in northern Arizona. Colonies were started along the Little Colorado, the Gila, the Salt and the San Pedro, and soon these settlements became models of planned communities. Some of the families active in the Mormon Church have entered state and national politics. No family has been more prominent in this regard than the descendants of David King Udall. Among them, Stewart Udall, Secretary of the Interior, and his brother, Morris, Congressman from Arizona, are well-known on the national scene.

Protestantism was later in coming to Arizona, but by the 1880's many churches had been built. The ministers who served in them were unusual men who were willing to put up the adobe bricks of their own churches. The services they conducted usually placed strong emphasis upon the exact words of the Bible and outlined a stern way of life for their congregations.

Although many Indians have accepted one of the religions introduced by the white man, they have also kept some of their own ancient religious heritage. Basically, nature worship underlies the structure of Indian belief. The propitiation of the elements for the common good is evident in their rituals. Mythology is ever present, and through it the origin of the world—its mountains and rivers—and the creation of man are explained.

Along with education and religion, the law came to the Arizona frontier, and there it was modified by prevailing conditions. Danger of Indian attack combined with the uncertainties of road travel caused men to carry firearms. Skill with guns was a fact of life and yet the six-shooter was hardly as prominent as Western movies and television would indicate. Laws covered the carrying of guns and local law officers were responsible for preserving the peace. They gave careful scrutiny to armed strangers. In spite of such measures, however, street fights and murders were not infrequent. Most people became used to the sound of gunfire at any hour of the day or night.

With long distances between towns and the transient nature of the population, renegades and fugitives had an advantage in Arizona over law enforcement officers. The countryside offered countless opportunities for conccalment of criminals and evasion of officers. This gave the outlaws a sense of bravado and a contempt for law.

Most Arizona towns at one time or another had to resort to vigilante groups to secure law-enforcement. In the spirit of the frontier this was not repulsive; rather it was a practical device to administer punishment where regular law enforcement had failed or was not available.

Because of an unruly element which often congregated in boom towns, the task of pioneer judges was not easy. Lonely stretches of road offered opportunities to stage bandits. Rustlers found sanctuary in the caves and canyons of large unsettled areas between towns. The judges coped valiantly with the problems inherent in such conditions in spite of methods that frequently were informal and unorthodox by legalistic standards.

Law enforcement in the territory was made more difficult by the presence of great mineral wealth which attracted not only good men, but bad. Racketeers, horsethieves, gunmen and gamblers mingled with lawyers, doctors, ministers and laborers on a frontier where life was one of the cheapest commodities.

Tales of gold and silver strikes had excited American interest in the Southwest back in the days of Spanish control. The Mexican period, which was a time of great unruliness, saw mining neglected. Mountain men, however, probed the area for pelts and gold and perhaps even from curiosity and they confirmed reports of great mineral wealth available to those willing to brave the Apache menace.

During the American period Poston was the first great promoter of Arizona mining. His operations in Tubac were extensive but the deteriorating conditions and the Civil War blighted progress. Gold placers along the Colorado and Gila and fabulous discoveries near Prescott and along the Hassayampa made prospectors out of ordinary men.

The age of the great silver bonanzas was heralded by the Tombstone discovery in 1877. Silver remained king until the electrical business created a large copper market. The copper interest then went into ascendancy in the mining activity in Arizona. Copper is found chiefly in an area called the Copper Province which fans out from Tucson in a great circle with a radius of about 100 miles. At first only high grade ore was processed, but scientific research has now made practical the processing of low-grade ore which twenty-five years ago would have been discarded.

With the influx of people seeking wealth from mines were those who came to supply the needs of settlers. Among them was Michel Goldwater. He came to La Paz and operated a large wholesale and retail business. Later he expanded his operations, opening stores in Phoenix, Parker and Prescott. This early merchant was the grandfather of Arizona's only Presidential candidate, Barry Goldwater. The family has always been active in Arizona's development.

A merchant and freighter who operated further to the south was

Estéban Ochoa. His business was thriving when the Confederate occupation of Tucson brought it to a halt. Estéban had to choose between cooperation or exile. He hesitated not a moment to choose the latter. After the Union take-over he was back in business on a larger scale than before.

After 1863, servicing of the many mining communities brought a boom to all freighters and merchants. In the process, in the western end of the territory, steamboat traffic on the Colorado surged ahead. By the 1880's the spanning of the territory by two transcontinental railroads revolutionized transportation and provided the key to the economic development of the interior of the territory. A network of short lines appeared and these served communities that would otherwise have been isolated.

Although mining became Arizona's major industry, the post-Civil War period saw new markets for beef in Arizona and beyond its boundaries. The numerous army posts and Indian reservations required great quantities and Uncle Sam had no peer as a purchaser. Then, when rail transport came, Arizona beef found more distant markets. Cattle raising went through three phases in Arizona. At first cattle were run on the open range, but after barbed wire made its appearance stockmen had better control of their herds. The third stage in the cattle business came when windmills pumped water to the ranges and with a constant water supply ranchers began to work for improved animals.

Cattlemen seemed to have a chronic dislike for sheepmen, possibly because of an erroneous idea that cattle could not graze where sheep have been. The worst range war in Arizona was the Pleasant Valley War in the Tonto Basin in 1887, which brought fear and death into a large area.

All during this long, troubled territorial period, citizens clamored for admission as a state into the American Union. Repeatedly Washington turned a cold shoulder to Arizona. Many reasons were given for this refusal. Some felt that Eastern senators were afraid of the Western bloc which represented only one third of the people of the nation. Others saw the need for a source of appointive patronage jobs for the party in power. Many said that Arizona was too sparsely settled, its population largely Indian, Mexican, and criminal, and not fit for American statehood. Arizona had to wait forty-nine years for this honor.

During that time the location of the capital shifted several times. In 1867 it left Prescott for Tucson, and returned ten years later. Then in 1889 it found its permanent home in Phoenix. During the territorial years, there were seventeen appointed governors, most of them Republicans who did not become permanent residents of the territory. Most of them served Washington first and Arizona second. Many of them used the post in Arizona only as a stop-gap until some better job turned up. Pioneer citizens chafed under this situation for many of them and their friends had been forced, time and again, to face tragedy and death on this frontier. They longed for orderly government which would give them full participation in the government of the United States.

In 1891 the fight for statehood became more militant than ever. The Indian Wars were over; two transcontinental railroads crossed the area; population was increasing; schools and newspapers were functioning realities; the presence of vast mineral wealth guaranteed the economy. Citizens of Arizona Territory felt that statehood could no longer be denied them. Nevertheless, years of wrangling debate and a frustrating counter-proposal, joint statehood with New Mexico, would have to be voted down before they could achieve their goal.

By 1910 the climate for success in the statehood controversy began to look quite favorable. Arizona, however, under the influence of the Progressive sentiment sweeping the West at that time, wrote a liberal constitution, embracing initiative, referendum and recall. The latter measure applied to every public office in the state of Arizona. Since this included judges, President William Howard Taft, himself a conservative former judge, refused to accept it. In no mood to lose this opportunity for statehood, Arizona bowed in submission to Taft's dictum and removed recall of judges from its document. Taft, using a golden pen, on February 14, 1912, signed the proclamation that made Arizona the 48th state of the American Union.

Books to Read

Bailey, Paul D., *Jacob Hamblin, Buckskin Apostle* (Los Angeles: Westernlore, 1948) tells how Mormon missionary work has carried on through colonizing. Breakenridge, William M., *Helldorado* (Boston: Houghton Mifflin, 1928) describes the bringing of law to Cochise County; Clelland, Robert Glass, *A History of Phelps Dodge, 1834–1950* (New York: Alfred A. Knopf, 1952); Dobie, James Frank, *Apache Gold and Yaqui Silver* (Boston: Little, Brown & Co., 1939) contains stories of buried treasure and lost mines; Dunning, Charles and Edward Peplow, *Rock to Riches* (Phoenix: Southwest Publishing Co., 1959) is the only easy-to-read history of mining in Arizona; Faulk, Odie (editor), *John Baptiste Salpointe, Soldier of the Cross* (Tucson: Diocese of Tucson, 1966), a segment of the earlier account by Salpointe. *Soldier of the Cross,* covers missionary work in the Southwest after the Mexican War; Forrest, Earle R., *Arizona's Dark and Bloody Ground.* (Caldwell, Idaho: Caxton Press, 1959) is an exceedingly readable account of the Pleasant Valley War; Gustafson, A. M., (editor), *John Spring's Arizona* (Tucson, University of Arizona Press, 1966), largely a reprint of articles which appeared in a Washington, D. C. newspaper in 1902 and 1903, recalls life in Arizona during the early territorial period; Hinton, Richard J., *The Handbook to Arizona.* (Tucson: Arizona Silhouettes, 1954, reprint), a mass of information on the natural resources of Arizona and their development up to 1877; Hodge, Hiram C., *Arizona as it Was, 1877* (Chicago: Rio Grande Press, 1962, reprint) describes missions, mines, agriculture, natural resources, Indians, schools; Hopkins, Ernest J., and Alfred Thomas, Jr. *The Arizona State University Story*

(Phoenix: Southwest Publishing Co., 1960) ; Keithley, Ralph, *Buckey O'Neill* (Caldwell, Idaho: Caxton Press, 1949), biography of a lawman on the frontier; Kelly, George H., *Legislative History, Arizona 1864–1912* (Phoenix: Manufacturing Stationers, 1926) ; Lamar, Howard Roberts, *The Far Southwest, 1846–1912: A Territorial History* (New Haven: Yale University Press, 1966), see especially Part 4 which describes Arizona and its emergence to statehood; Martin, Douglas, *The Lamp in the Desert: The Story of the University of Arizona* (Tucson: University of Arizona Press, 1960) and also by Martin is a collection of items which appeared in this historic newspaper during territorial days, *Tombstone's Epitaph* (Albuquerque: University of New Mexico Press, 1958) ; Miller, Joseph, *Arizona Cavalcade* (New York: Hastings House, 1962) contains a wide range of topics, taken from the files of early newspapers; and also taken from early newspaper articles is Miller's *The Last Frontier* (New York: Hastings House, 1956) ; Murbarger, Nell, *Ghosts of the Adobe Walls* (Los Angeles: Westernlore, 1964), compendium for travel in Arizona describing ghost towns; Myers, John Myers, *The Last Chance: Tombstone's Early Years* (New York; E. P. Dutton and Co., 1950) is a most accurate account of early Tombstone; Nelson, Pearl Udall, *Arizona Pioneer Mormon, David King Udall* (Tucson: Arizona Silhouettes, 1959) history of a prominent Mormon family; Powell, Donald, *The Peralta Grant* (Norman: University of Oklahoma Press: 1960), story of a gigantic hoax; Quebbeman, Frances E., *Medicine in Territorial Arizona* (Phoenix: Arizona Historical Foundation, 1966), pioneer medicine in early Arizona; Rockfellow, John A., *Log of an Arizona Trailblazer* (Tucson: Arizona Silhouettes, 1955, reprint) on ranching in Cochise stronghold; Theobald, John and Lillian, *Arizona Territorial Post Offices and Post Masters* (Phoenix: Arizona Historical Foundation, 1961) ; Wagoner, Jay J., *History of the Cattle Industry in Southern Arizona, 1540–1940* (Tucson: University of Arizona Social Science Bulletin #20, 1952), published Master's Thesis.

Places to Visit

Arizona Museum: In Phoenix. Many exhibits featuring life in territorial period.

Arizona Pioneers' Historical Society: Excellent collection of pioneer memorabilia. Wealth of documentary material in library available to the public. Free admission. 949 East 2nd Street, Tucson. Monday through Friday 8 A.M. to 5 P.M.; Saturday 8 A.M. to 1 P.M.; Sunday (in winter) 2 P.M. to 5 P.M.

Jerome State Historical Park: Old mining town with an exciting history. Tour of abandoned mining complex. Dioramas, display of mining equipment. Admission to mining museum, adults 25¢.

Prescott: Many memorials of territorial days. Group of early buildings in Pioneer Square. Sharlott Hall Museum.

Tombstone: Whole town an exhibit featuring colorful past. The Birdcage Theatre, Crystal Palace Saloon, O K Corral site, Schieffelin Hall, Boot Hill Grave Yard and the Court House.

Wickenburg: Several sites of historical significance: the Jail Tree, the old Stage Station, the Vulture mine and the place of the Wickenburg Massacre. From Wickenburg to Ehrenberg on the Colorado the Trail of Graves where many perished from thirst.

Yuma Territorial Prison State Historic Park: Exciting tour. Interesting museum: abandoned cell block, dungeons and prison graveyard. Open daily 8 A.M. to 5 P.M. Admission: Adults, 25¢.

Progress Since Statehood
1912-1968

FEBRUARY 14, 1912, the birthday of the state, ushered in a period of high optimism. After half a century of territorial tutelage Arizonans at last had the privilege of full citizenship in the United States. Within nine months, they exercised their prerogative, restoring to their constitution the recall of judges which had been a bone of contention with President Taft.

One reason for reassurance about the days ahead was the completion the year before of the great Theodore Roosevelt Dam on the Salt River. This was the first national irrigation project under the National Reclamation Act of 1902. The very next year, the Salt River Valley Water Users Association was formed to undertake sound plans for financing the great dam, and projects associated with it.

In 1906 the first foundation stone was laid and the mighty structure arose in a wilderness site unbelievably difficult of access. Five years later the dam, 284 feet high, 184 feet thick at the base, tapering to 16 feet at the top, was ready for its dedication. The popular ex-President, Teddy Roosevelt, traveled to the site for the ceremony. Appropriately named for him, for he had been in office when the Reclamation Act became law, Roosevelt Dam was the first of many storage dams for Arizona.

The Granite Reef Diversion Dam had already been finished and canals diverted water to the fields on both sides of the Salt and distribution systems were in operation. Controlled dispersion of water to the fertile central valley where sub-tropical temperatures prevail made agriculture a major item in the economy of the new state. The small, dusty capital city of Phoenix became a verdant mecca which in fifty years multiplied its 1912 population by forty.

Water has been the key to this phenomenal growth.

Need for water storage, flood control and increased hydro-electric power has brought a vast expansion of dam building. As a part of the Salt River Project, the Salt and Verde rivers have been harnessed and the loss of their water through seasonal floods has been checked. The system of water control in the central valley is a model worthy of the widest emulation.

Coolidge Dam, named for another ex-President, crosses the Gila near Globe and is the first large multiple dome dam ever built. The story goes that at the dedication ceremony in 1930 the humorist, Will Rogers, noting more grass than water in the lake as it began to fill, remarked "If this was my lake, I'd mow it."

The greatest source of water in Arizona lies in the mighty Colorado which runs for hundreds of miles through the state and forms much of its western boundary. The first important structure built on it after the passage of the National Reclamation Act was upstream from Yuma, the Laguna Dam, completed in 1907. This installation diverts water to canals from which the water is syphoned to the Arizona side of the river to fields around Yuma.

The tremendous operation which envisioned the harnessing of the Colorado, however, was Hoover Dam built on the Arizona-Nevada boundary at a cost of over $100 million. The huge structure, 730 feet above bedrock impounds Lake Mead, which is over a hundred miles long. Hoover Dam provides no irrigation water for Arizona but it protects numerous such projects further downstream. Arizona shares in the revenue from its power and in the recreation facilities on Lake Mead.

Upstream from this giant installation is the new Glen Canyon Dam which impounds Lake Powell, a two-hundred mile recreation facility. Like Hoover, Glen Canyon Dam provides a giant power plant. Many economic benefits have accrued to Arizona through the construction of this $400-million dam.

In addition to these huge installations working to counteract aridity, the passage into law of the Central Arizona Project will control the water of the Colorado River by the construction of a system of dams, aqueducts, pumping stations, large reservoirs and long pipelines. Large dams at Bridge and Marble Canyon will be a part of the system. The proposal encountered violent opposition from Arizona's neighbors who also claimed the Colorado's waters for their own uses. California had for many years quarreled over any plan to divert water to Arizona. Through its larger population it has tried to block the Central Arizona Project in the House of Representatives. In a recent Supreme Court decision Arizona won the right to an increased share in the Colorado's water. Finally, the project was passed in 1968 by the 90th Congress.

The Central Arizona Project advocates no expansion of agricultural acreage but rather the maintenance of a viable economy which is threatened with a shortage of water for the fastest growing state in the Union. If its expansion of water control facilities is permitted to continue, Arizona might well find dam construction listed among its major industries in its second half century as a state.

Besides irrigation development Arizona's economy was aided by war orders which came from World War I. Employment increased in the mines and Arizona became the leader in the nation in output of copper. This was due to the development of low-grade copper deposits which required large invested capital. Only big companies could undertake installations required for this type of operation. Profits exceeded even the fondest dreams of the investors and production was pushed to the maximum.

Arizona received a great economic stimulus from World War I but it was to suffer a swift reaction after the war ended. By 1920 mining operations were curtailed; the price of copper dropped sharply. In the collapse of the cotton market the price plummeted from a dollar a pound to nothing. Cattlemen also had a serious setback caused by a severe drought. Although the downward turn was relieved by a few years of more stable economic conditions, the worldwide depression which struck after the 1929 stock market collapse did not exempt Arizona from its blight.

In 1933 the many agencies of the New Deal brought federal spending into the Arizona business picture. The Works Progress Administration provided jobs in a great variety of projects which today bear the imprint W.P.A. Many mines had been shut down during the early years of this decade, but major companies kept skeleton crews on their payrolls. Later on, the war in Europe affected the situation favorably and the economy improved.

As the nation moved into a war economy to aid the allies against Hitler, employment and trade in the whole country, and accordingly in Arizona, rose to prosperity levels. The Phelps Dodge Company had by this time become the largest copper producer in the world. Most copper locations in Arizona came within the scope of its attention.

The cotton business, so depressed in 1920, underwent a change in the 1930's. Farmers developed a short-staple variety of cotton that did well in Arizona. While other farming dropped off alarmingly, cotton planting was heavy and the price improved from 5½¢ to 12¢ a pound in 1936. Cotton was of major importance to the economy because at this time the entire crop was sold outside the state, and it was sometimes referred to as the "precious crop."

During the early 1930's the price of beef was so low that cattle-men at times gave away their young calves rather than raise them. Federal purchases for the relief program helped keep the business going and vast range improvement by the federal government encouraged the stockmen.

The Civilian Conservation Corps performed a valiant service. The training of large numbers of young men in soil conservation and forestry in twenty-seven camps in the state produced a lasting effect upon the forests and rangelands of Arizona.

Whether the New Deal policies instituted during the Franklin D. Roosevelt year, alone might ever have pulled the country out of the Great Depression will never be positively known. War orders came toward the end of the decade and with them came prosperity to both the country and to Arizona. The 1940's brought boom times. Mines reached new, high levels of production. Farms were operating full-scale to feed war-torn Europe.

The three C's—Copper, Cotton and Cattle—which long had been a gauge to Arizona's economic picture, by this time had to recognize the significance of another C, the salubrious Climate. Increasingly people were recognizing that Arizona had potential as a health, retirement and tourist center.

The government also took climate into consideration when it established many air bases and other training centers in Arizona. This brought thousands of military personnel and their families to swell the population of the 48th state. Many of these became permanent residents after the war. Industries with government contracts for aviation supplies, seeing an advantage in the protected inland location, set up plants in Arizona. Many of their workers remained when some of the factories ceased operating at the end of the war.

The decade of the 1950's started with a population 50 per cent greater than at the beginning of the previous decade. This increase caused a tremendous boom in the building trade and some other branches of Arizona's economy. It also aided in bringing manufacturing into the state permanently, providing the necessary labor force. To attract more manufacturing for the future, changes were made in the tax laws to encourage it. By 1956 manufacturing had moved into first place in the state's economy. While businesses connected with aviation were established, there were also many plants for making machine tools, electronic devices, weapons, missile parts and countless other items. Arizona in this decade emerged as an area attractive to management with pleasant living conditions for workers.

By 1960, population in Arizona had increased by 74 per cent over that of 1950. Tourism was bringing hundreds of millions of dollars into the economy. The spirit of the Old West has been preserved in countless Dude Ranches which feature simple living, horseback riding and rodeos for guests from around the globe. Winter resorts near some of the larger cities are fully equipped with facilities for vacation living. With the assets of a delightful winter climate and many unusual scenic attractions, this industry seems to have an assured future.

Retirement communities recently built in Arizona bring every convenience and comfort, and a dash of fun as well, to senior citizens for whom they have been established. This group of citizens is showing a high percentage rate of increase in relation to the state's total population growth.

With a half century of struggle for a star in the American flag behind her, Arizona embarked upon her search for an identity in the family of states. With manufacturing, agriculture, mining and tourism pouring wealth into her economy, Arizona's bright future seems assured.

Books to Read

Statistics on Arizona's economic growth and tables showing comparative population statistics have been published by the Employment Security Commission of Arizona, *Arizona: Century of Growth* (Phoenix: Employment Commission, 1963); Fuchs, James R., *A History of Williams, Arizona, 1876–1951.* (Social Science Bulletin No. 23, Nov. 1953) (Tucson: University of Arizona Press, 1955), Published Master's Thesis; Mann, Dean E., *The Politics of Water in Arizona* (Tucson: University of Arizona Press, 1963); Mason, Bruce B. and H. R. Hink, *Constitutional Government in Arizona* (Tempe: Arizona State University, 1963); Moore, Daniel G., *Log of a Twentieth Century Cowboy* (Tucson: University of Arizona Press, 1965) contains a brief glossary and description of some ranches and their brands; Morey, Roy D., *Politics and Legislation: The Office of Governor of Arizona.* (Tucson: University of Arizona Press, 1965) explains the governor's role in Arizona government; Sparks, George F., (editor), *A Many Colored Toga* (Tucson: University of Arizona Press, 1962), diary of Senator Henry Fountain Ashurst from the gaining of statehood to the New Deal; Stevens, Robert Conway, *A History of Chandler, Arizona, 1912–1953* (Social Science Bulletin, No. 25, Oct. 1954) (Tucson: University of Arizona Press, 1955) published Master's Thesis; Terrell, John Upton, *War for the Colorado River,* vol. 1, *The California-Arizona Controversy* (Glendale, Calif.: Arthur H. Clark, 1965); Van Petten, Donald R., *The Constitution and Government in Arizona* (Phoenix: Sun Country Publishing Co., 1952), an historical account of the erection of the state government.

Places to Visit

Brewery Gulch Gazette: Building at Bisbee is open to visitors. It has a sign which reads "The sun shines on Brewery Gulch 330 days in the year but there is moonshine every day."

Lavender Pit: In Bisbee. Covers 155 acres. The Phelps Dodge Company is said to have invested 25 million in it to deliver the first pound of copper.

The Kitt Peak Observatory: In the Papago Reservation, 53 miles southwest of Tucson. Self-contained community with all necessary utilities. Contains the world's largest telescope for solar observation as well as other telescopes and astronomical equipment.

Lowell Observatory: At Flagstaff, on Mars Hill. Has been a world famous center of astronomical research.

Sacramento Pit: At Bisbee. Man-made crater, 435 feet deep, with copper, green and rust-colored walls. Before abandonment, mine yielded almost 21-million tons of ore in fourteen years.

The State Capitol: At Phoenix. Arrangements may be made for school groups to visit legislature.

Local facilities such as courts, council meetings, police stations, weather bureaus, newspaper plants, airports and other transportation facilities may be visited.

Trips may be arranged to the dams and powerhouses in the respective areas. On the Salt River: Theodore Roosevelt, Horse Mesa, Mormon Flat and Stewart Mountain dams; on the Verde: Bartlett and Horseshoe; on the Gila: Coolidge dam and Wellton-Mohawk Irrigation Project; on the Colorado: Hoover, Davis, Parker and Glen Canyon dams.

In various localities guided tours for interested groups are furnished by mines, dairies, bakeries, slaughterhouses, bottling companies, radio and television stations, manufacturing plants, farms, newspaper plants and numerous others. Through such visits the study of local history may become more meaningful.

Teachers College Press
Teachers College, Columbia University
New York, New York